PITMAN SHORTERHAND DICTIONARY

GEORGE A. REID
Chairman, Business Education Department
The Faculty of Education, University of Toronto

Edited by MARION ANGUS
Business Education Consultant
Pitman Publishing

Copp Clark Pitman
A division of Copp Clark Limited
Toronto

ISBN 0-7730-4229-6

AUSTRALIA—Pitman Publishing Pty. Ltd., Melbourne
U.K.—Pitman Publishing Ltd., London
NEW ZEALAND—Pitman Publishing, New Zealand Ltd.
U.S.A.—Fearon-Pitman Publishers Inc., Belmont, California
EAST AFRICA—Sir Isaac Pitman Ltd., Nairobi, Kenya
SOUTH AFRICA—Pitman Publishing Co. SA (Pty.) Ltd., Johannesburg

Copp Clark Pitman
517 Wellington Street West
Toronto, Ontario
M5V 1G1

Printed and bound in Canada

PREFACE

This *Pitman Shorterhand Dictionary* has been prepared to meet the immediate needs of students, teachers and writers of Pitman Shorterhand for a work of reference that will provide the correct shorthand outlines for most of the frequently used words in the language.

This dictionary is a selected list of words and is not intended in any way to be comprehensive since only the words themselves and their shorthand outlines are given. The Publisher's purpose has been to produce a representative and, in the main, non-technical list of English words that are in common use, or that are likely to be used in dictation across a wide variety of activities in business, industry, the professions and authorship. Inevitably the choice of words for inclusion will not cover all requirements within the bounds of a volume containing between 16 000 and 17 000 entries, but it is hoped that the selection made will satisfy most day-to-day needs.

The list of place names includes all countries in the world and their capitals, and all the larger cities in major countries, especially those in Australasia, Canada, the United States and the British Isles. Many adjectives of nationality are also included.

All the pacers and most of the derivatives in Pitman Shorterhand are shown italicized in the main list and as a complete alphabetical list on page 233. A list of common metric units and their derivatives is included.

The list of proper names is highly selective and is restricted to those most commonly in use.

In order to include as many different words and outlines as possible, repetition has been avoided. For example, a proper name that is also a common word will usually appear in the main list only, and where a town name occurs in more than one country it is included in the list of place names once only. Many surnames are also common words and therefore are to be found in the main list.

Most plurals, present participles and past tenses, unless irregular, are excluded, since the shorthand outlines for these are formed on the regular pattern of circle S, the dot -ing, or the disjoined T or D, but the reader should remember that in some cases a derivative exists where, say, a present tense would rarely if ever be used. In these cases, the derivative is given. However, because shorthand outlines for comparatives, superlatives and adverbs differ, most adjectives are included with their derivatives.

Most homonyms and words with the same spelling but different meanings and pronunciations are included.

Shaded vowel signs appear in this dictionary to conform with the international version of Pitman Shorterhand, entitled Pitman 2000. Slight differences in vowel shading will not be significant to North American students of Shorterhand who do not use this principle, but will meet the needs of international Shorterhand writers.

The writer of Pitman Shorterhand will find it possible to write the shorthand outline for every word in the English language simply by following the rules of the system. It is our belief that as a result of using the *Pitman Shorterhand Dictionary,* all writers of Pitman Shorterhand will increase their basic vocabularies, will read more fluently from printed shorthand, and consequently will write their shorthand outlines with greater speed and confidence.

CONTENTS

A

a	abnormal	absence
		absense
abandon	abnormally	absent
abate	aboard	absentee
abattoir	abode	absolute
abbey	abolish	absolutely
abbreviate	abolition	absolve
abbreviation	abominable	absorb
abdicate	aboriginal	absorbent
abdomen	abortive	absorption
abdominal	abound	abstain
abduct	about	abstainer
abduction	abrasion	abstention
abeyance	abrasive	abstinence
abhor	abreast	abstract
abhorrence	abridge	abstraction
abhorrent	abroad	abstruse
abide	abrogate	absurd
ability	abrogation	absurdity
ablaze	abrupt	absurdly
able	abruptly	abundance
able-bodied	abruptness	abundant
ablution	abscess	abundantly
ably	abscond	abuse

1

abusive		acclaim		accuracy	
abusively		acclamation		accurate	
abysmal		acclimatize		accurately	
abyss		accommodate		accusation	
academic		accommodation		accusative	
academy		accompani-ment		accuse	
accede		accompanist		accustom	
accelerate		accompany		ace	
acceleration		accomplice		acetylene	
accelerator		accomplish		ache	
accent		accomplishment		achieve	
accentuate		accord		achievement	
accentuation		accordance		acid	
accept		according		acidity	
acceptable		accordingly or		acknowledge	
acceptance		accost		acknowledge-ment	
access		account		acorn	
accessibility		accountable		acoustics	
accessible		accountancy		acquaint	
accession		accountant		acquaintance	
accessory		accrue		acquiesce	
accident		accumulate		acquiescence	
accidental		accumulation		acquire	
accidentally		accumulator		acquisition	

2

acquisitive		acutely		adherent		
acquit		adage		adhesion		
acquittal		adamant		adhesive		
acre		adapt		adieu		
acreage		adaptability		adjacent		
acrid		adaptable		adjective		
acrimonious		adaptation		adjoin		
acrimoniously		adapter		adjourn		
across		add		adjournment		
acrylic		adder		adjudicate		
act		addict		adjust		
action		addiction		adjustment		
actionable		addition		adjutant		
activate		additional		administer		
active		additionally		administrate		
actively		additive		administration		
activity		address		administrative		
actor		addressee		administratively		
actress		adept		administrator		
actual		adequacy		admirable		
actually		adequate		admiral		
actuary		adequately		Admiralty		
acumen		adhere		admiration		
acute		adherence		admire		

3

admirer		advancement		advocacy	
admissible		advantage		advocate	
admission		advantageous		aerial	
admit		advantageously		aerodrome	
admittance		advantages		aerodynamics	
admittedly		adventitious		aeronautic	
admonish		adventure		aeroplane	
adolescence		adventurer		aerosol	
adolescent		adventuress		aerospace	
adopt		adverb		aesthetic	
adoption		adversary		affability	
adorable		adverse		affable	
adoration		adversely		affably	
adore		adversity		affair	
adorn		advertise		affect	
adornment		advertisement		affectation	
adrenalin		advertiser		affection	
adrift		advice		affectionate	
adroit		advisability		affectionately	
adsorb		advisable		affidavit	
adulation		advise		affiliate	
adult		advisedly		affiliation	
adultery		adviser		affinity	
advance		advisory		affirm	

4

affirmative		aggravate		aground		
affix		aggravation		ah		
afflict		aggregate		ahead		
affliction		aggregation		aid		
affluence		aggression		ail		
afford		aggressive		ailment		
affront		aggressively		aim		
afloat		aggressor		aimless		
aforesaid		aggrieve		aimlessly		
afraid		aghast		air		
afresh		agile		airborne		
after		agility		aircraft		
aftermath		agitate		airfield		
afternoon		agitation		airily		
afterthought		agitator		airline		
afterwards		agnostic		airmail		
again		ago		airman		
against		agonizing		airway		
age		agony		airworthy		
ageless		agree		aisle		
agency		agreeable		ajar		
agenda		agreement		akin		
agent		agricultural		alabaster		
aggrandizement		agriculture		alacrity		

5

alarm	allay	*almost*
alas	allegation	alms
albeit	allege	alone
albumen	allegiance	along
alcohol	allegory	alongside
alcoholic	allergic	aloof
alcove	alleviate	aloud
alderman	alley	alphabet
ale	alliance	aphabetical
alert	allocate	alphabetically
alertness	allocation	alpine
alfalfa	allot	already
alias	allotment	*also*
alibi	allow	altar
alien	allowable	alter
alienate	allowance	alteration
alienation	alloy	alternate, *v*
alight	allude	alternate, *adj*
align aline	allure	alternately
alignment alinement	alluringly	alternative
alike	ally	alternatively
alimony	almighty	although
alive	almond	altitude
all	almoner	*altogether*

altruistic	ambush	amphibious
aluminium	ameliorate	ample
aluminum	amen	amplification
always	amenable	amplifier
am	amend	amplify
amalgamate	amendment	amply
amalgamation	amenity	amputate
amass	amiable	amputation
amateur	amiably	amuse
amaze	amicable	amusement
amazement	amicably	*an*
amazingly	amid	anachronism
ambassador	amidst	anaemia / anemia
amber	amiss	anaemic / anemic
ambidexterous	ammunition	anaesthetic / anesthetic
ambient	amnesty	anagram
ambiguity	among	analogous
ambiguous	amongst	analogy
ambiguously	amoral	analyse / analyze
ambition	amorous	analysis
ambitious	amorously *or*	analyst
ambitiously	amorphous	analytic
amble	amount	analytical
ambulance	ampersand	analytically

7

anarchist	anguish	annually
anarchy	angular	annuity
anathema	angularity	annul
anatomical	animal	annum
anatomy	animate	anoint
ancestor	animation	anomalous
ancestral	animosity	anomaly
anchor	animus	anonymity
anchorage	aniseed	anonymous
anchovy	ankle	anonymously
ancient	annals	another
and	annexation	answer
anecdote	annexe annex	answerable
anemometer	annihilate	ant
anew	annihilation	antagonism
angel	anniversary	antagonist
anger	annotate	antagonistic
angle	annotation	antagonize
angler	announce	antecedent
Anglican	announcement	antedate
anglicize	announcer	anthem
Anglo-Saxon	annoy	anthology
angrily	annoyance	anthrax
angry	annual	anthropology

8

antibiotic	anyhow	appeal
antic	anyone	appear
anticipate	*anything*	appearance ... or
anticipation	anyway	appease
anticlimax	anywhere	append
anticlockwise	apart	appendage
anticyclone	apartment	appendices
antidote	apathetic	appendicitis
antipathy	apathy	appendix
antipodes	ape	appendixes
antiquarian	aperture	appertain
antiquated	apex	appetite
antique	apiece	appetize
antiquity	apologetic	applaud
antiseptic	apologize	applause
antisocial	apology	apple
antithesis	apostle	appliance
antler	apostrophe	applicable
anvil	appal	applicant
anxiety	apparatus	application
anxious	apparel	apply
anxiously	apparent	appoint
any	apparently	appointment
anybody	apparition	apportion

apposite	approximate	archaic
appraisal	approximately	archbishop
appraise	approximation	archery
appreciable	April	archipelago
appreciably	apron	architect
appreciate	apropos	architectural
appreciation	apt	architecture
appreciative	aptitude	archives
apprehend	aptly	ardent
apprehension	aptness	ardently
apprehensive	aquarium	ardour ardor
apprehensively	aquatic	arduous
apprentice	aqueduct	are
apprenticeship	arable	area
apprise	arbiter	arena
approach	arbitrarily	argue
approachable	arbitrary	argument
approbation	arbitrate	argumentative
appropriate	arbitration	arid
appropriately	arbitrator	aridity
appropriation	arc	arise
approval	arcade	arisen
approve	arch	aristocracy
approvingly	archaeology	aristocrat

10

aristocratic		arrogance		asbestos			
arithmetic		arrogant		ascend			
ark		arrogantly		ascendancy			
				ascendency			
arm		arrow		ascent			
armament		arsenal		ascertain			
armature		arsenic		ascribe			
armchair		arson		ash			
armistice		art		ashamed			
armour		arterial		ashore			
armor							
armoury		artery		aside			
army		artful		ask			
aroma		artfully		askance			
aromatic		arthritis		askew			
arose		article		asleep			
around		articulate		aspect			
arouse		artificial		asphalt			
arraign		artificially		asphyxia			
arrange		artillery		aspirant			
arrangement		artisan		aspirate, *n*			
array		artist		aspirate, *v*			
arrear		artistic		aspiration			
arrest		artistically		aspire			
arrival		artless		ass			
arrive		*as*		assail			

11

assailant	assistant	astutely	
assassin	assizes	asunder	
assassinate	associate	asylum	
assault	association	at	
assay	assort	ate	
assemble	assortment	atheism	
assembly	assume	athlete	
assent	assumption	athletic	
assert	assurance	atlas	
assertion	assure	atmosphere	
assess	assuredly	atmospheric	
assessment	asterisk	atom	
assessor	asthma	atomic	
asset	astonish	atone	
assiduously	astonishment	atonement	
assign	astound	atrocious	
assignation	astray	atrociously	
assignee	astride	atrocity	
assignment	astringent	attach	
assignor	astrologer	attachment	
assimilate	astronaut	attack	
assimilation	astronomer	attain	
assist	astronomy	attainable	
assistance	astute	attainment	

12

attempt		audaciously		author	
attend		audacity		authoress	
attendance		audibility		authoritative	
attendant		audible		authoritatively	
attention		audibly		authority	
attentive		audience		authorization	
attentively		audio-typist		authorize	
attest		audio-visual		authorship	
attestation		audit		auto	
attester attestor		audition		autobiography	
attic		auditor		autocracy	
attire		auditorium		autocrat	
attitude		aught		autocratic	
attorney		augment		autograph	
attract		August		automatic	
attraction		aunt		automatically	
attractive		auspices		automation	
attractively		auspicious		automobile	
attributable		auspiciously		autonomy	
attribute		austere		autopsy	
auburn		austerity		autumn	
auction		authentic		auxiliary	
auctioneer		authenticate		avail	
audacious		authenticity		availability	

available		avid		away	
avalanche		avidly		awe	
avarice		avocado		awful	
avenge		avoid		awkward	
avenue		avoidable		awkwardly	
average		avoidance		awning	
averse		await		awoke	
aversion		awake		axe	
avert		awaken		ax axiom	
aviation		award		axle	
aviator		aware		azure	

B

baby	bake	banana
babyish	baker	band
bachelor	bakery	bandage
back	balance	bandit
backbencher	balance-sheet	bandstand
background	balcony	bandwagon
backhanded	bald	bandy
backlash	balderdash	bane
backlog	baldly	bang
backwards	bale	banish
bacon	ball	banishment
bacteria	ballad	banister
bad	ballast	bank
bade	ballet	banker
badge	ballistics	bankrupt
badly	balloon	bankruptcy
baffle	ballot	banner
bag	balm	banns
baggage	balmy	banquet
bail	balsam	baptism
bailey	bamboo	baptize
bailiff	ban	bar
bait	banal	barbarian

15

barber		barter		baton	
barbican		base		battalion	
barbiturate		baseball		batten	
bard		baseboard		batter	
bare		baseless		battery	
barefaced		basement		battle	
barely		bash		battle-axe	
bargain		bashful		battlefield	
barge		bashfully		battleship	
bark		basic		bauxite	
barley		basically		bawl	
barn		basin		bay	
barometer		basis		bayonet	
barometric		bask		bazaar	
baron		basket		be	
baroness		basketball		beach	
barrack		baste		beacon	
barrage		bastion		bead	
barrel		bat		beak	
barren		batch		beam	
barrenness		bath		bean	
barricade		bathe		bear	
barrier		bather		bearable	
barrow		bathroom		beard	

16

bearer	bedstead	begin
beast	bedtime	beginner
beastly	bee	begrudge
beat	beech	beguile
beaten	beef	begun
beau	beehive	behalf
beautician	beeline	behave
beautiful	been	behaviour behavior
beautifully	beer	behead
beautify	beeswax	beheld
beauty	beet	behind
beaver	beetle	behold
became	beetroot	beholder
because	befall	behoove
beckon	befallen	beige
become	befell	being
bed	befit	belated
bedcover	*before*	belfry
bedding	*before*hand	belief
bedeck	befriend	believable
bedouin	beg	believe
bedridden	began	believer
bedrock	beget	belittle
bedroom	beggar	bell

belligerent	benighted	betray
bellow	benign	betrayal
belly	benignant	betroth
belong	benignly	betrothal
belovèd	bent	better
below	bequeath	betterment
belt	bequest	between
bemoan	berate	betwixt
bench	bereave	beverage
bend	bereavement	bevy
beneath	bereft	beware
benediction	beret	bewilder
benefactor	berry	bewilderment
benefactress	berth	bewitch
benefice	beseech	beyond
beneficence	beset	biannual
beneficent	beside	bias
beneficial	besiege	bib
beneficially	besmirch	Bible
beneficiary	besought	biblical
benefit	best	bibliography
benevolence	bestial	biceps
benevolent	bestow	bicker
benevolently	bet	bicycle

bid	binoculars	bivouac
bidder	biographer	bizarre
biennial	biographical	black
big	biography	blackberry
bigamist	biological	blackbird
bigamy	biology	blackboard
bigger	bipartisan	blacken
biggest	birch	blackguard
bigot	bird	blackmail
bigotry	birth	blacksmith
bigwig	birthday	bladder
bile	birthmark	blade
bilge	birthplace	blame
bilingual	birthright	blameless
bilious	biscuit	blameworthy
biliousness	bisect	bland
bill	bishop	blandly
billet	bit	blank
billiards	bite	blanket
billion	bitten	blankly
billow	bitter	blare
binary	bitterness	blaspheme
bind	bitumen	blast
binder	bituminous	blatant

blatantly		blister		blue		
blaze		blithe		bluebell		
bleach		blithely		blueberry		
bleak		blithesome		blue-*eyed*		
bleat		blitz		bluff		
bled		blizzard		blunder		
bleed		bloated		blunt		
bleep		block		bluntly		
blemish		blockade		blur		
blend		blockhead		blurb		
bless		blond blonde		blurt		
blessèd		blood		blush		
blest		bloodthirsty		bluster		
blew		bloom		boar		
blight		blossom		board		
blind		blot		boarder		
blindfold		blotch		boast		
blindly		blotter		boastful		
blindness		blotting-paper		boastfulness		
blink		blouse		boat		
bliss		blow		bob		
blissful		blown		bobbin		
blissfully		blubber		bobsleigh		
blissfulness		bludgeon		bode		

20

bodily		bond		boost		
body		bondage		booster		
boffin		bone		boot		
bog		boneless		booth		
bogey		bonfire		border		
boggle		bonnet		bore		
bogus		bonus		bored		
boil		booby		boredom		
boiler		book		born		
boisterous		bookbinder		borne		
boisterously		bookcase		borough		
bold		bookkeeper		borrow		
bolder		bookkeeping		borrower		
boldest		booklet		bosom		
boldly		bookmaker		boss		
boldness		bookmark		botanist		
bollard		bookseller		botany		
bolster		bookshelf		botch		
bolt		bookstall		both		
bomb		bookstore		bother		
bombard		bookworm		bothersome		
bombastic		boom		bottle		
bomber		boon		bottleneck		
bombshell		boor		bottom		

21

boudoir	boyhood	brave
bough	boyish	bravely
bought	boyishly	bravery
boulder bowlder	brace	brawl
boulevard	bracelet	brawn
bounce	bracken	bray
bound	bracket	brazen
boundary	brackish	brazenly
boundless	brag	breach
bountiful	braid	bread
bounty	Braille	breadth
bouquet	brain	breadwinner
bourgeois	brainless	break
bout	brainwash	breakable
bow, *n*	braise	breakage
bow, *v*	brake	breakdown
bowels	bran	breakfast
bower	branch	breakwater
bowl	brand	breast
bowler	brandish	breath
box	brandy	breathe
boxer	brash	breathless
boy	brass	bred
boycott	bravado	breech

22

breed		brighter		broadest	
breeder		brightest		broadly	
breeze		brightly		broadminded	
breezily		brightness		brocade	
breezy		brilliance		brochure	
brethren		brilliancy		brogue	
brevity		brilliant		broil	
brew		brilliantly		broke	
bribe		brim		broken	
bribery		brimful		brokenhearted	
brick		brine		broker	
bricklayer		bring		bromide	
bridal		brink		bronchial	
bride		brinkmanship		bronchitis	
bridegroom		brisk		bronze	
bridge		briskly		brooch	
bridle		bristle		brood	
brief		brittle		broody	
briefcase		broach		brook	
briefly		broad		broom	
brigade		broadcast		broth	
brigand		broadcasting		brother	
bright		broaden		brotherhood	
brighten		broader	or	brother-*in*-law	

23

brought	buddy	bulletin
brow	budge	bullet-proof
browbeat	budget	bullion
brown	buff	bullock
browse	buffalo	bull's-*eye*
bruise	buffer	bully
brunette	buffet	bulwark
brunt	buffoon	bump
brush	bug	bumper
brushwood	buggy	bumpkin
brusque	bugle	bumptious
brusquely	bugler	bumptiousness
brutal	build	bun
brutality	builder	bunch
brutally	building	bundle
brute	build-up	bung
bubble	built	bungalow
buccaneer	bulb	bungle
buck	bulbous	bunk
bucket	bulge	bunker
buckle	bulk	bunting
buckwheat	bulky	buoy
bucolic	bull	buoyancy
bud	bullet	buoyant

buoyantly	burrow	butler
burble	bursar	butt
burden	burst	butter
burdensome	bury	button
bureau	bus	button-hole
bureaucracy	bush	buttress
burg	bushel	buxom
burgh	bushy	buy
burglar	busier	buyer
burglary	busiest	buzz
burial	busily	buzzer
burlesque	business	by, bye
burly	businesslike	by-election
burn	bust	bygone
burner	bustle	by-law, bye-law
burnish	busy	by-product
burnt	*but*	bystander
burr	butcher	byword

C

cab	calculable	cameo	
cabbage	calculate	camera	
cabin	calculation	cameraman	
cabinet	calculator	camouflage	
cable	caldron	camp	
cablegram	calendar	campaign	
cachet	calf	camphor	
cackle	calibration	campus	
cactus	calibre caliber	can	
cad	calico	canal	
cadence	call	canary	
cadet	caller	cancel	
cadge	callous	cancellation	
cadre	callow	cancer	
café	calm	candid	
cafeteria	calmly	candidacy	
cage	calorie	candidate	
cairn	calumny	candidature	
cajole	cam	candidly	
cake	camber	candle	
calamitous	cambric	candlestick	
calamity	came	candour candor	
calcium	camel	candy	

26

cane	capacity	caravan	
canine	cape	carbide	
canister	capillary	carbine	
canker	capital	carbolic	
cannibal	capitalist	carbon	
cannon	capitalization	carbonic	
cannot	capitalize	carburettor	
canoe	capitation	carcass	
canon	capitulate	card	
canopy	caprice	cardboard	
cant	capricious	cardiac	
can't	capsize	cardigan	
canteen	capsule	cardinal	
canter	captain	cardiogram	
canton	caption	care	
canvas	captivate	career	
canvass	captivation	careful	
canvasser	captive	carefully	
canyon	captivity	careless	
cap	captor	carelessly	
capability	capture	carelessness	
capable	car	caress	
capably	caramel	caret	
capacious	carat	caretaker	

27

careworn		cascade		cataract	
cargo		case		catarrh	
caricature		casework		catastrophe	
caries		cash		catastrophic	
carnival		cashew		catch	
carnivorous		cashier		catchment	
carol		cashmere		catchword	
carouse		casino		categorize	
carpenter		cask		category	
carpentry		casket		cater	
carpet		cassette		caterpillar	
carriage		cast		cathedral	
carrier		caste		cathode	
carrot		castigate		catholic	
carry		cast-iron		catholicism	
cart		castle		cattle	
cartage		castor		caught	
carte blanche		casual		cauldron	
cartel		casualty		cauliflower	
carton		casuistry		cause	
cartoon		cat		caustic	
cartoonist		cataclysm		cauterize	
cartridge		catalogue catalog		caution	
carve		catapult		cautionary	

28

cautious	cellulose	cereal
cautiously	Celtic	ceremonial
cavalcade	cement	ceremonially
cavalry	cemetery	ceremonious
cave	censor	ceremony
cavern	censorship	certain
cavil	censure	certainly
cavity	cent	certainty
cease	centenary	certificate
ceaseless	centennial	certification
ceaselessly	centigrade	certify
cedar	centigram	cessation
cede	centilitre	cession
ceiling	centime	cesspit
celebrate	centimetre	chafe
celebration	centipede	chaff
celebrity	central	chagrin
celery	centralization	chain
celestial	centralize	chair
celibacy	centrally	chairman
celibate	centre center	chairmanship
cell	centrifugal	chalet
cellar	century	chalk
celluloid	ceramics	challenge

29

challenger	charade	chatter
chamber	charcoal	chauffeur
champagne	charge	chauvinist
champion	chargeable	cheap
championship	chariot	cheapen
chance	charismatic	cheaper
chancel	charitable	cheapest
chancellor	charitably	cheaply
chancery	charity	cheapness
change	charlatan	cheat
changeable	charm	check
changeless	charred	checker
channel	chart	checkout
chant	charter	cheek
chaos	chase	cheep
chaotic	chasm	cheer
chaotically	chassis	cheerful
chap	chaste	cheerfully
chapel	chasten	cheerfulness
chaperon	chastise	cheerless
chaplain	chastisement	cheéry
chapter	chastity	cheese
character	chat	cheeseparing
characteristic	chattel	chef

chemical		chill		choke		
chemist		chilly		cholera		
chemistry		chime		choose		
cheque		chimney		chop		
cheque-book check-book		chimpanzee		chopper		
cherish		chin		choral		
cherry		china		chord		
cherub		chink		chore		
chess		chip		chorister		
chest		chiropodist		chorus		
chestnut		chirp		chose		
chevron		chisel		chosen		
chew		chit		Christ		
chic		chivalrous		christen		
chicken		chivalry		Christendom		
chide		chloride		Christian		
chief		chlorine		Christianity		
chiefly		chloroform		Christmas		
child		chock		chromatic		
childhood		chocolate		chromium		
childish		choice		chromosome		
childishly		choicer		chronic		
childless		choicest		chronicle		
children		choir		chronological		

31

chronologically	circular	civilian
chrysalis	circularize	civility
chrysan-themum	circulate	civilization
chubby	circulation	civilize
chuck	circumference	clad
chum	circumlocution	claim
chunk	circumscribe	claimant
church	circumspect	clairvoyance
churchyard	circumspection	clairvoyant
churlish	circumstance	clamber
churlishly	circumstantial	clammy
churn	circumstantially	clamour clamor
chute	circumvent	clamp
cider	circus	clan
cigar	cist	clandestine
cigarette	cistern	clang
cinch	citadel	clap
cinder	citation	claret
cinema	cite	clarification
cinematograph	citizen	clarify
cipher	citizenship	clarion
circle	city	clarionet
circuit	civic	clarity
circuitous	civil	clash

32

clasp	clearing house	climber
class	clearly	clinch
classic	clearness	cling
classical	clear-sighted	clinic
classification	cleave	clinical
classify	cleft	clinically
classmate	clemency	clink
classroom	clench	clinker
clatter	clergy	clip
clause	clergyman	clique
claustrophobia	cleric	cloak
claw	clerical	clock
clay	clerk	clockwork
clean	clerkship	clod
cleaner	clever	clog
cleanest	cliché	cloister
cleanliness	click	close
cleanly	client	closely
cleanse	clientele	closet
cleanser	cliff	close-up
clear	climate	closure
clearance	climatic	clot
clearer	climax	cloth
clearest	climb	clothe

cloud	coarsen	coercion
clover	coast	coeval
clown	coaster	coexist
cloy	coastguard	coffee
club	coastline	coffer
clubhouse	coat	cog
cluck	coax	cogent
clue	coaxial	cogently
clump	cobber	cogitate
clumsily	cobbler	cogitation
clumsy	cobweb	cognac
clung	cocaine	cohere
cluster	cock	coherence
clutch	cockney	coherent
clutter	cocktail	cohesion
coach	cocoa	cohesive
coagulate	coconut	coiffure
coal	cocoon	coil
coalesce	cod	coin
coal-field	coddle	coinage
coalition	code	coincide
coal-mine	codicil	coincidence
coarse	codify	coke
coarsely	coerce	cold

34

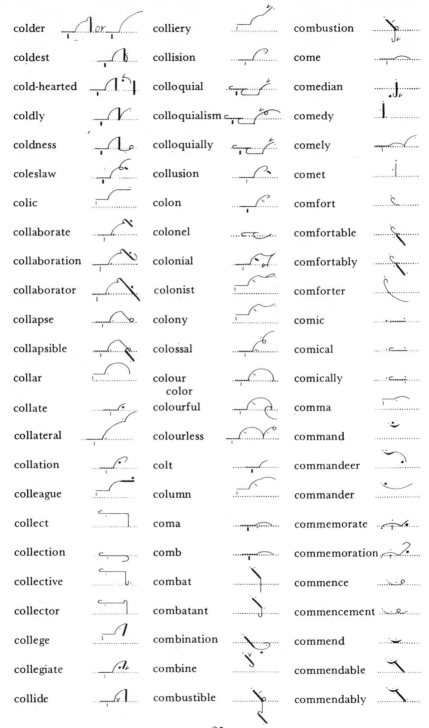

colder	colliery	combustion
coldest	collision	come
cold-hearted	colloquial	comedian
coldly	colloquialism	comedy
coldness	colloquially	comely
coleslaw	collusion	comet
colic	colon	comfort
collaborate	colonel	comfortable
collaboration	colonial	comfortably
collaborator	colonist	comforter
collapse	colony	comic
collapsible	colossal	comical
collar	colour color	comically
collate	colourful	comma
collateral	colourless	command
collation	colt	commandeer
colleague	column	commander
collect	coma	commemorate
collection	comb	commemoration
collective	combat	commence
collector	combatant	commencement
college	combination	commend
collegiate	combine	commendable
collide	combustible	commendably

35

commendation	commonwealth	compatibility
commensurate	commotion	compatible
comment	communicate	compel
commentary	communication	compendium
commerce	communion	compensate
commercial	communism	compensation
commercialize	communist	compete
commercially	community	competence
commiserate	commute	competent
commissar	commuter	competently
commission	compact	competition
commissioner	companion	competitive
commit	companionship	competitively
commitment	company	competitor
committal	comparable	compilation
committee	comparative	compile
commodious	comparatively	compiler
commodity	compare	complacency
common	comparison	complacent
commoner	compartment	complacently
commonest	compass	complain
commonly	compassion	complainant
commonplace	compassionate	complaint
commonsense	compassionately	complement

complementary	comprehend	conceivably
complete	compre- hensible	conceive
completely	comprehension	concentrate
completeness	comprehensive	concentration
completion	compress	concentric
complex	compression	concept
complexion	compressor	conception
complexity	comprise	concern
compliance	compromise	concert
compliant	compulsion	concession
complicate	compulsive	conciliate
complication	compulsively	conciliation
complicity	compulsorily	conciliatory
compliment	compulsory	concise
complimentary	compunction	concisely
comply	computation	conciseness
component	compute	conclude
compose	computer	conclusion
composer	comrade	conclusive
composite	concave	conclusively
composition	conceal	concoct
compositor	concede	concoction
composure	conceit	concord
compound	conceivable	concourse

concrete		conductor		conflagration	
concur		conduit		conflict	
concurrence		cone		confluence	
concurrent		confection		conform	
concurrently		confectioner		conformity	
concussion		confectionery		confound	
condemn		confederate		confront	
condemnation		confederation		confuse	
condemnatory		confer		confusion	
condensation		conference		confute	
condense		confess		congeal	
condenser		confession		congenial	
condescend		confidante		congenially	
condescension		confide		congenital	
condign		confidence		congestion	
condiment		confident		conglomeration	
condition		confidential		congratulate	
conditional		confidently		congratulations	
conditionally		confine		congregate	
condole		confinement		congregation	
condolence		confirm		congregational	
condone		confirmation		congress	
conducive		confiscate		congressional	
conduct		confiscation		congressman	

38

conical	consecrate	consignor
conifer	consecration	consist
conjecture	consecutive	consistency
conjugal	consecutively	consistent
conjugate	consensus	consistently
conjunction	consent	consolation
conjunctive	consequence	console
conjuncture	consequent	consolidate
conjure	consequential	consolidation
connect	consequently	consonant
connection connexion	conservation	consonantal
connivance	conservative	consort
connive	conservatively	consortium
connoisseur	conserve	conspectus
connotation	consider	conspicuous
conquer	considerable	conspicuously
conqueror	considerably	conspiracy
conquest	considerate	conspire
conscience	considerately	constable
conscientious	consideration	constant
conscientiously	consign	constantly
conscious	consignee	constellation
consciously	consigner	consternation
consciousness	consignment	constituency

39

constituent	consumption	contentiously
constitute	consumptive	contentment
constitution	contact	contest
constitutional	contagion	contestant
constitutionally	contagious	context
constrain	contain	contiguous
constraint	container	continent
constrict	contaminate	continental
constriction	contamination	contingency
construct	contemplate	contingent
construction	contemplation	contingently
constructive	contem- poraneous	continual
constructively	contemporary	continually
construe	contempt	continuance
consul	contemptible	continuation
consular	contemptibly	continue
consulate	contemptuous	continuity
consult	contemptuously	continuous
consultant	contend	continuously
consultation	contender	contort
consultative	content	contortion
consumable	contentedly	contour
consume	contention	contra
consumer	contentious	contraband

40

contract	controversially	convertible
contraction	controversy	convex
contractor	conundrum	convey
contractual	convalescence	conveyance
contractually	convalescent	conveyor
contradict	convector	convict
contradiction	convene	conviction
contradictory	convenience	convince
contraption	convenient	convivial
contrarily	conveniently	convoke
contrary	convent	convoy
contrast	convention	convulse
contravene	conventional	convulsion
contribute	conventionally	cook
contribution	converge	cooker
contributor	conversant	cookery
contributory	conversation	cool
contrite	conversational	cooler
contrivance	conversationally	coolest
contrive	converse	cool-headed
control	conversely	co-operate
controllable	conversion	co-operation
controller	convert	co-operative
controversial	converter	co-operatively

41

co-operator	core	correspond
co-opt	co-respondent	correspondence
co-ordinate	cork	correspondent
co-ordination	corkscrew	corridor
copartnership	corn	corroborate
cope	corner	corroboration
copious	corollary	corroborative
copiously	coronary	corrode
copper	coroner	corrosion
copse	corporate	corrosive
copy	corporation	corrugated
copy-book	corps	corrupt
copyhold	corpse	corruption
copyright	corpulence	cosh
copy-writer	corpulent	cosmetic
coquettish	corpus	cosmic
coral	corral	cosmopolitan
cord	correct	cost
cordage	correction	costliness
cordial	corrective	costly
cordiality	correctly	costume
cordially	correctness	cosy
cordon	correlate	cot
corduroy	correlation	coterie

cottage	counting-house	cover
cotton	countless	coverage
couch	country	covert
cough	countryman	covet
could	countryside	covetous
council	county	coxswain
councillor councilor	coup	cow
counsel	coupé	coward
counsellor counselor	couple	cowardice
count	coupon	cowardly
countenance	courage	cow-hide
counter	courageous	coy
counteract	courageously	cozily
counter-balance	courier	cozy
counter-blast	course	crab
counter-claim	court	crack
counterfeit	courteous	crackle
counter-feiter	courteously	cradle
counterfoil	courtesy	craft
countermand	court-house	craftily
counterpart	courtroom	craftiness
countersign	courtyard	craftsman
counter-vailing	cousin	crafty
countess	covenant	crag

43

cram		credential		crevice	
cramp		credibility		crew	
cranberry		credible		crib	
crane		credibly		cricket	
crank		credit		crime	
crash		creditable		criminal	
crass		creditably		criminally	
crate		creditor		crimson	
crater		credulity		cringe	
crave		credulous		crinkle	
crawl		creed		cripple	
crayon		creek		crisis	
craze		creep		crisp	
crazy		cremate		criterion	
creak		creole		critic	
cream		creosote		critical	
crease		crepe		critically	
create		crept		criticism	
creation		crescent		criticize criticise	
creative		crest		critique	
creatively		crestfallen		croak	
creator		cretaceous		crochet	
creature		cretin		crockery	
credence		cretonne		crocodile	

44

croft		crude		cuckoo		
crony		crudity		cucumber		
crook		cruel		cuddle		
crooked		cruelly		cudgel		
crookedly		cruelty		cue		
crop		cruise		cuff		
cropper		cruiser		cuisine		
croquet		crumb		culinary		
cross		crumble		culminate		
cross-breed		crumple		culmination		
cross-examination		crunch		culpable		
cross-examine		crusade		culprit		
crossly		crush		cult		
crossroads		crust		cultivate		
crossword		crutch		cultivation		
crotchet		crux		cultural		
crouch		cry		culturally		
crow		crypt		culture		
crowd		crystal		cumbersome		
crown		crystallize		cumulative		
crucial		cub		cumulatively		
crucifix		cube		cuneiform		
crucifixion		cubic		cunning		
crucify		cubicle		cunningly		or

45

cup	cursèd	cut	cute
cupboard	cursive	cute	
curable	cursorily	cutlery	
curate	cursory	cutlet	
curb	curt	cut-out	
cure	curtail	cutter	
curfew	curtailment	cyanide	
curio	curtain	cycle	
curiosity	curtly	cyclical	
curious	curvature	cyclist	
curiously	curve	cyclone	
curl	cushion	cylinder	
curly	custard	cylindrical	
currant	custodian	cynic	
currency	custody	cynical	
current	custom	cynically	
currently	customarily	cynicism	
curricula	customary	cynosure	
curriculum	customer	cypher	
curry	custom-house	cyst	
curse	customs	cytology	

D

dab	danger	dawn
dabble	dangerous	day
Dad	dangerously	daybreak
Daddy	dangle	daylight
daily	dare	daytime
daintily	daringly _or_	daze
dainty	dark	dazzle
dairy	darken	dead
dais	darker	deaden
daisy	darkest	deadline
dale	darkness	deadlock
dam	darling	deadly
damage	darn	deaf
damask	dart	deafen
dame	dash	deal
damp	dashboard	dealer
dampen	data	dealt
damper	date	dean
dampness	daub	_dear_
damsel	daughter	dearer
dance	daunt	dearest
dancer	dauntless	dearly
dandy	dawdle	dearth

47

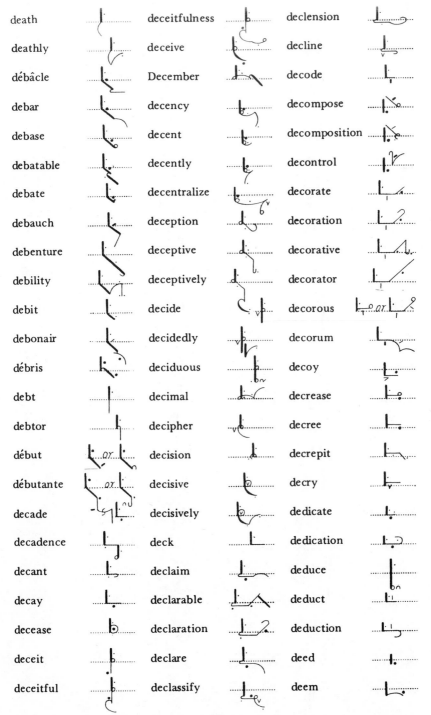

death	deceitfulness	declension
deathly	deceive	decline
débâcle	December	decode
debar	decency	decompose
debase	decent	decomposition
debatable	decently	decontrol
debate	decentralize	decorate
debauch	deception	decoration
debenture	deceptive	decorative
debility	deceptively	decorator
debit	decide	decorous
debonair	decidedly	decorum
débris	deciduous	decoy
debt	decimal	decrease
debtor	decipher	decree
début	decision	decrepit
débutante	decisive	decry
decade	decisively	dedicate
decadence	deck	dedication
decant	declaim	deduce
decay	declarable	deduct
decease	declaration	deduction
deceit	declare	deed
deceitful	declassify	deem

48

deep		defiance		degradation	
deepen		defiant		degrade	
deeper		deficiency		dehydrate	
deepest		deficient		deity	
deeply		deficiently		deject	
deface		deficit		dejection	
defacement		define		delay	
defamation		definite		delectable	
defamatory		definitely		delegate	
defame		definition		delegation	
default		definitive		delete	
defect, *v*		deflate		deletion	
defect, *n*		deflation		deliberate, *v*	
defective		deflect		deliberate, *adj*	
defence defense		deform		deliberation	
defenceless		deformity		delicacy	
defend		defraud		delicate	
defendant		defray		delicious	
defensible		deft		delight	
defensive		deftly		delightful	
defensively		defunct		delightfully	
defer		defy		delimitation	
deference		degenerate, *v*		delineate	
deferment		degenerate, *adj*		delinquency	

49

delinquent		demote		department	
delirious		demur		departmental	
deliver		demure		departmentally	
deliverance		demy		departure	
delivery		denial		depend	
delude		denier		dependable	
deluge		denigrate		dependably	
delusion		denim		dependant	
demand		denomination		dependence	
demarcate		denomina- tional		dependency	
demeanour demeanor		denote		dependent	
demise		denounce		depict	
democracy		dense		deplete	
democrat		densely		depletion	
democratic		density		deplorable	
democratically		dent		deplore	
demon		dental		deploy	
demonstrable		dentist		deport	
demonstrate		dentistry		deportment	
demonstration		denture		depose	
demonstrative		denude		deposit	
demonstratively		denunciation		depository	
demonstrator		deny		depot	
demoralize		depart		deprave	

50

depravity	descend	desk
deprecate	descendant	desolate
depreciate	descent	desolation
depreciation	describe	despair
depress	description	despatch
depression	descriptive	desperate
deprivation	descriptively	desperately
deprive	desecrate	desperation
depth	desecration	despicable
deputation	desegregate	despise
depute	desert	despite
deputize	deserter	despondency
deputy	desertion	despondent
derelict	deserve	despotic
dereliction	deservedly	despotism
deride	design	dessert
derision	designate	destination
derisive	designation	destine
derivation	designer	destiny
derivative	desirability	destitute
derive	desirable	destitution
dermatitis	desire	destroy
dermatology	desirous	destroyer
dervish	desist	destruction

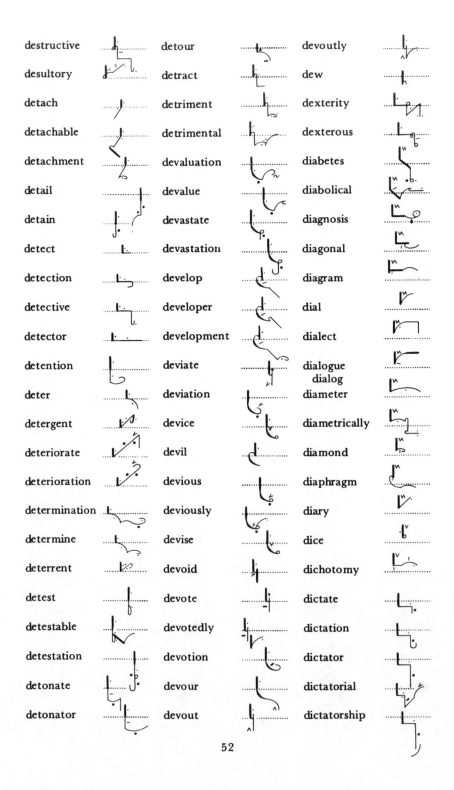

destructive	detour	devoutly	
desultory	detract	dew	
detach	detriment	dexterity	
detachable	detrimental	dexterous	
detachment	devaluation	diabetes	
detail	devalue	diabolical	
detain	devastate	diagnosis	
detect	devastation	diagonal	
detection	develop	diagram	
detective	developer	dial	
detector	development	dialect	
detention	deviate	dialogue dialog	
deter	deviation	diameter	
detergent	device	diametrically	
deteriorate	devil	diamond	
deterioration	devious	diaphragm	
determination	deviously	diary	
determine	devise	dice	
deterrent	devoid	dichotomy	
detest	devote	dictate	
detestable	devotedly	dictation	
detestation	devotion	dictator	
detonate	devour	dictatorial	
detonator	devout	dictatorship	

52

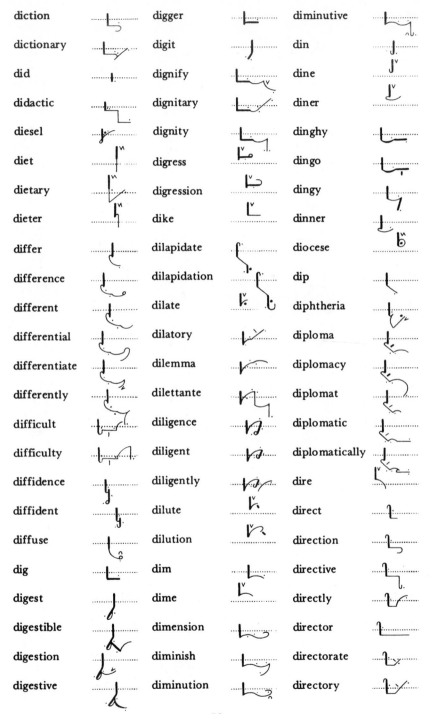

diction	digger	diminutive
dictionary	digit	din
did	dignify	dine
didactic	dignitary	diner
diesel	dignity	dinghy
diet	digress	dingo
dietary	digression	dingy
dieter	dike	dinner
differ	dilapidate	diocese
difference	dilapidation	dip
different	dilate	diphtheria
differential	dilatory	diploma
differentiate	dilemma	diplomacy
differently	dilettante	diplomat
difficult	diligence	diplomatic
difficulty	diligent	diplomatically
diffidence	diligently	dire
diffident	dilute	direct
diffuse	dilution	direction
dig	dim	directive
digest	dime	directly
digestible	dimension	director
digestion	diminish	directorate
digestive	diminution	directory

53

dirge	disavow	discount	
dirt	disbelieve	discourage	
dirty	disburse	discouragement	
disability	disbursement	discourse	
disable	disc disk	discover	
disabuse	discard	discovery	
disadvantage	discern	discredit	
disaffected	discernible	discreditable	
disagree	discernment	discreet	
disagreeable	discharge	discreetly	
disagreement	disciple	discrepancy	
disappear	discipline	discretion	
disappearance	disclaim	discriminate	
disappoint	disclose	discursive	
disappointment	disclosure	discus	
disapprobation	discolour discolor	discuss	
disapproval	discomfort	discussion	
disarm	discommode	disdain	
disarmament	disconnect	disease	
disarrange	disconsolate	disembark	
disarray	discontent	disem- barkation	
disaster	discontinue	disenchanted	
disastrous	discord	disenfranchise	
disastrously	discordant	disengage	

54

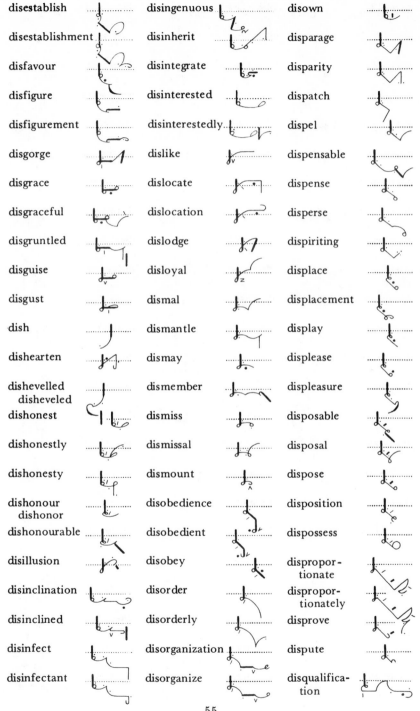

disestablish

disestablishment

disfavour

disfigure

disfigurement

disgorge

disgrace

disgraceful

disgruntled

disguise

disgust

dish

dishearten

dishevelled
disheveled
dishonest

dishonestly

dishonesty

dishonour
dishonor
dishonourable

disillusion

disinclination

disinclined

disinfect

disinfectant

disingenuous

disinherit

disintegrate

disinterested

disinterestedly

dislike

dislocate

dislocation

dislodge

disloyal

dismal

dismantle

dismay

dismember

dismiss

dismissal

dismount

disobedience

disobedient

disobey

disorder

disorderly

disorganization

disorganize

disown

disparage

disparity

dispatch

dispel

dispensable

dispense

disperse

dispiriting

displace

displacement

display

displease

displeasure

disposable

disposal

dispose

disposition

dispossess

dispropor-
tionate

dispropor-
tionately

disprove

dispute

disqualifica-
tion

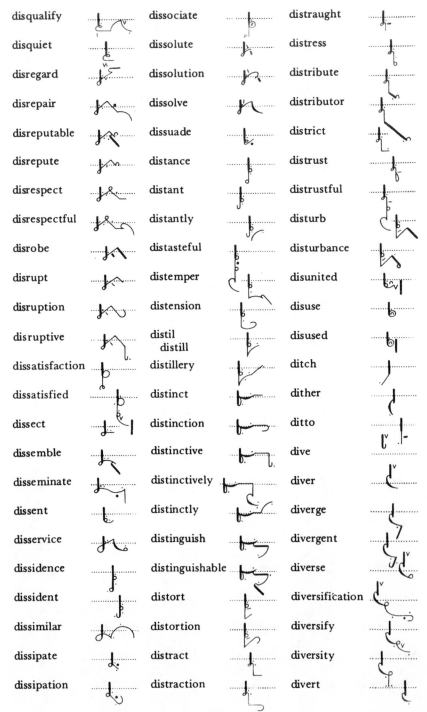

disqualify	dissociate	distraught
disquiet	dissolute	distress
disregard	dissolution	distribute
disrepair	dissolve	distributor
disreputable	dissuade	district
disrepute	distance	distrust
disrespect	distant	distrustful
disrespectful	distantly	disturb
disrobe	distasteful	disturbance
disrupt	distemper	disunited
disruption	distension	disuse
disruptive	distil distill	disused
dissatisfaction	distillery	ditch
dissatisfied	distinct	dither
dissect	distinction	ditto
dissemble	distinctive	dive
disseminate	distinctively	diver
dissent	distinctly	diverge
disservice	distinguish	divergent
dissidence	distinguishable	diverse
dissident	distort	diversification
dissimilar	distortion	diversify
dissipate	distract	diversity
dissipation	distraction	divert

divest		documentation		donate	
divide		dodge		donation	
dividend		does		done	
divine		doff		donkey	
divinely		dog		donor	
divinity		dogfight		doom	
divisible		doggerel		door	
division		dogma		doorway	
divisional		dogmatic		dope	
divisive		dole		dormant	
divorce		doleful		dormitory	
divulge		doll		dosage	
dizzily		*dollar*		dose	
dizzy		dolphin		dossier	
do		dolt		dot	
docile		domain		dotage	
docker		dome		double	
docket		domestic		doubly	
dockyard		domicile		doubt	
doctor, Dr.		dominant		doubtful	
doctrinal		dominate		doubtfully	
doctrine		domination		doubtingly	
document		domineer		doubtless	
documentary		dominion		dough	

doughnut	dramatist	drew	
doughty	drank	dried	
dour	drape	drier	
douse	drapery	drift	
dove	drastic	drill	
dowdy	drastically	drily	
down	draught	drink	
downcast	draughty	drinker	
downfall	draw	drip	
downhearted	drawback	drive	
downhill	drawer	drivel	
downpour	drawl	driven	
downright	drawn	driver	
downstairs	dray	drizzle	
downwards	dread	drone	
doze	dreadful	droop	
dozen	dream	drop	
drab	dreamt	drop-out	
dragon	dreary	drought	
drain	dredge	drove	
drainage	drench	drown	
drake	dress	drowsiness	
drama	dresser	drowsy	
dramatically	dressmaker	drudge	

58

drudgery		duel		duration		
drug		duet		duress		
druggist		dug		during		
druid		duke		dusk		
drum		dull		dusky		
drummer		duly		dust		
drunk		dumb		duster		
drunkard		dumbfounded		dutiful		
drunken		dummy		duty		
drunkenness		dump		dwarf		
dry		dun		dwell		
dryer		dunce		dweller		
dual		dune		dwelt		
dubious		dungeon		dwindle		
dubiously		dupe		dye		
duck		duplicate		dyer		
duckling		duplication		dynamic		
duct		duplicator		dynamite		
ductile		duplicity		dynamo		
dud		durability		dynasty		
due		durable		dyspepsia		

E

each	Easter	eddy
eager	eastern	edge
eagerly	eastward	edgeways
eagle	easy	edible
ear	eat	edict
earache	eaten	edification
earl	eaves	edifice
earlier	ebb	edify
earliest	ebony	edit
early	ebullient	edition
earn	eccentric	editor
earnest	eccentricity	editorial
earnestly	ecclesiastic	editorially
earth	echo	editorship
earthenware	eclipse	educate
earthly	economic	education
earthquake	economical	educational
ease	economically	educationally
easel	economist	educator
easier	economize	Edwardian
easiest	economy	eerie
easily	ecstasy / extasy	eerily
east	ecumenical	efface

60

effacement		eight	_8 or 1_	electric	
effect		eighteen	_18 or 1_	electrically	
effective		eighteenth	_18(or 1_	electricity	
effectively		eighth	_8(or 1_	electrification	
effectiveness		eightieth	_80(or 1_	electrify	
effectual		eighty	_80 or 1_	electrode	
effeminate		either		electrolysis	
effeminately		ejaculate		electronic	
effervesce		eject		elegance	
efficacious		eke		elegant	
efficiency		elaborate, _v_		elegantly	
efficient		elaborate, _adj_		element	
efficiently		elaborately		elementary	
effigy		elaboration		elephant	
effluent		elapse		elevate	
effort		elastic		elevation	
effrontery		elasticity		elevator	
effusive		elated		eleven	_11 or_
egalitarian		elbow		eleventh	_11(or 1_
egg		elder		elicit	
ego		eldest		eligibility	
egotistical		elect		eligible	
eh		election		eliminate	
eider-down		electorate		elimination	

elite	embarrassment	eminence
Elizabethan	embassy	eminent
ellipsis	embellish	eminently
elocution	embezzle	emissary
elongate	embezzlement	emit
elope	embezzler	emollient
eloquence	embitter	emolument
eloquent	emblem	emotion
eloquently	embody	emperor
else	embolism	emphasis
elsewhere	embrace	emphasize
elucidate	embrocation	emphatic
elude	embroider	emphatically
elusive	embroidery	empire
elusively	embryo	empirical
emaciate	embryonic	empirically
emanate	emendation	employ
emancipate	emerald	employee
emancipation	emerge	employer
embank- ment	emergency	employment
embargo	emetic	empower
embark	emigrant	empress
embarkation	emigrate	empty
embarrass	emigration	emu

62

emulate		endless		enhance	
emulation		endlessly		enigma	
emulsify		endorse		enigmatic	
emulsion		endorsement		enigmatically	
enable		endow		enjoin	
enact		endowment		enjoy	
enactment		endurable		enjoyable	
enamel		endurance		enjoyment	
enamour enamor		endure		*enlarge*	
enchant		enemy		*enlargement*	
encircle		energetic		*enlarger*	
enclose		energetically		enlighten	
enclosure		energy		enlightenment	
encounter		enervate		enlist	
encourage		enfold		enlistment	
encouragement		enforce		enliven	
encroach		enforcement		enmity	
encumber		engage		enormity	
encyclopaedia		engagement		enormous	
end		engine		enormously	
endanger		engineer		enough	
endear		engrave		enquire	
endeavour endeavor		engraver		enquiry	
endemic		engross		enrage	

63

enraptured		entirely		epic	
enrich		entirety		epicure	
enrol enroll		entitle		epidemic	
enrolment enrollment		entity		epilepsy	
ensemble		entomology		episcopal	
ensign		entourage		episode	
enslave		entrance		epistle	
ensnare		entrant		epitaph	
ensue		entreaty		epoch	
ensure		entrée		equable	
entail		entrepreneur		equal	
entangle		entrust		equality	
enter		entry		equalization	
enterprise		enumerate		equalize	
entertain		enunciate		equally	
entertainer		enunciation		equation	
entertainment		envelop		equator	
enthral		envelope		equatorial	
enthusiasm		enviable		equilibrium	
enthusiastic		envious		equinox	
enthusiastically		environment		equip	
entice		envoy		equipment	
enticement		envy		equitable	
entire		ephemeral		equitably	

equity		escape		ethical	
equivalent		escort		ethically	
equivocal		eskimo		ethics	
era		esoteric		ethos	
eradicate		especial		etiquette	
erase		especially		euphemism	
erect		espionage		euthanasia	
erection		esquire		evacuate	
erode		essay		evacuation	
erosion		essayist		evade	
erotic		essence		evaluate	
err		essential		evaluation	
errand		establish		evaporate	
errant		establishment		evasion	
erratic		estate		evasive	
erratically		esteem		evasively	
erroneous		estimate		eve	
erroneously		estimation		even	
error		estuary		evening	
erudite		et cetera, etc.		evenly	
erupt		eternal		event	
eruption		eternally		eventful	
escalate		eternity		eventual	
escapade		ethereal		eventuality	

eventually		exalt		excise	
ever		examination		excite	
evergreen		examine		excitement	
everlasting		examiner		exclaim	
everlastingly		example		exclamation	
every		exasperate		exclude	
everybody		excavate		exclusion	
everyone		excavation		exclusive	
every*thing*		exceed		exclusively	
everywhere		exceedingly		excommunicate	
evict		excel		excursion	
eviction		excellence		excusable	
evidence		excellent		excuse	
evident		excellently		execute	
evidently		except		execution	
evil		exception		executive	
evocative		exceptional		executor	
evolution		exceptionally		executrix	
evolve		excerpt		exemplary	
exacerbate		excess		exemplify	
exact		excessive		exempt	
exactly		excessively		exemption	
exaggerate		exchange		exercise	
exaggeration		exchequer		exert	

exertion		expanse		expiration		
exhale		expansion		expire		
exhaust		expansive		expiry		
exhaustion		expect		explain		
exhaustive		expectant		explanation		
exhibit		expectantly		explanatory		
exhibition		expectation		expletive		
exhibitor		expediency		explicit		
exhilarate		expedient		explicitly		
exhilaration		expediently		explode		
exhort		expedite		exploit		
exhortation		expedition		exploitation		
exhume		expel		exploration		
exile		expend		exploratory		
exist		expendable		explore		
existence		expenditure		explorer		
existent		expense		explosion		
exit		expensive		explosive		
exonerate		experience		exponent		
exorbitant		experiment		export		
exorcism		experimental		exporter		
exotic		experimen- tally		expose		
exotically		expert		exposition		
expand		expertly		exposure		

express		externally		extreme	
expression		extinct		extremely	
expressive		extinction		extremity	
expressly		extinguish		extricate	
expropriate		extinguisher		extrovert	
expulsion		extol		exuberance	
exquisite		extortion		exuberantly	
exquisitely		extra		exude	
extemporary		extract		exult	
extend		extraction		eye	
extension		extradite		eyeball	
extensive		extradition		eyebrow	
extensively		extraneous		eyelash	
extent		extraneously		eyelid	
extenuate		extra-ordinarily		eye-opener	
extenuation		extra-ordinary		eyesight	
exterior		extravagance		eyesore	
exterminate		extravagant		eye-strain	
external		extravagantly		eye-witness	

68

F

fable		failure		falter	
fabric		faint		fame	
fabrication		faintly		familiar	
fabulous		fair		familiarity	
façade		fairer		familiarization	
face		fairest		familiarize	
facetious		fairly		family	
facetiously		fairness		famine	
facial		fairy		famish	
facile		faith		famous	
facilitate		faithful		fan	
facility		faithfully		fanatic	
facsimile		faithless		fanatical	
fact		fake		fanaticism	
faction		fall		fanciful	
factor		fallacious		fancy	
factory		fallacy		fantastic	
factual		fallen		fantastically	
factually		false		fantasy	
faculty		falsehood		far	
fade		falsely		farce	
Fahrenheit		falsification		farcical	
fail		falsify		fare	

farewell	father	feather
farm	father-*in*-law	feathery
farmer	fatherland	feature
farmhouse	fathom	February
farmyard	fatigue	fed
far-reaching	fatten	federal
farther	faucet	federation
farthest	fault	fee
fascinate	faultless	feeble
fascination	faulty	feed
fascism	favour favor	feel
fashion	favourable favorable	feet
fashionable	favourably favorably	feint
fashionably	favourite favorite	felicitate
fast	favouritism favoritism	felicity
fasten	fear	fell
fastener	fearful	fellow
faster	fearfully	fellowship
fastest	fearless	felon
fastidious	fearsome	felony
fatal	feasibility	felt
fatality	feasible	female
fatally	feast	feminine
fate	feat	fence

70

fend	feud	fierce
fender	feudal	fiercely
fennel	fever	fiercer
ferment	feverish	fiercest
fermentation	feverishly	fiery
fern	few	fifteen
ferocious	fewer	fifteenth
ferociously	fiancé(e)	fifth
ferocity	fiasco	fiftieth
ferry	fiat	fifty
fertile	fibre / fiber	fig
fertility	fibreglass	fight
fertilization	fibrositis	fighter
fertilize	fickle	figment
fertilizer	fiction	figurative
fervent	fictitious	figuratively
fervently	fiddle	figure
fervour / fervor	fidelity	figure-head
fester	fidget	filament
festival	fidgety	file
festivity	field	filibuster
fetch	fiend	fill
fete	fiendish	filler
fetter	fiendishly	fillet

film		finish		fishhook		
filter		finite		fishy		
filth		fire		fission		
filthy		firearms		fissure		
filtration		fireman		fist		
fin		fireplace		fit		
final		fireproof		fitful		
finale		fireside		fitment		
finality		fireworks		fitness		
finalize		firm		fitter		
finally		firmament		fittest		
finance		firmer		fittingly		
financial		firmest		five		
financially		firmly		fix		
financier		first		fixation		
find		first-aid		fixative		
finder		first-class		fixedly		
fine		first-hand		fixture		
finely		firstly		fizzle		
finer		first-rate		flabbergasted		
finesse		fiscal		flabby		
finest		fish		flaccid		
finger		fisher		flag		
fingerprint		fishery		flagon		

72

flagrant		flax		flit		
flagrantly		flay		float		
flair		flea		flock		
flake		fled		flog		
flamboyant		flee		flood		
flame		fleece		floor		
flange		fleet		flop		
flank		flesh		floral		
flannel		flew		florid		
flannelette		flex		florist		
flap		flexibility		floss		
flapper		flexible		flotation		
flare		flick		flotsam		
flash		flicker		flounce		
flask		flight		flounder		
flat		flimsy		flour		
flatly		flinch		flourish		
flatten		fling		flout		
flatter		flint		flow		
flattery		flip		flower		
flaunt		flippant		flowery		
flavour flavor		flippantly		flown		
flaw		flirt		fluctuate		
flawless		flirtatious		fluctuation		

73

flue		focus		foolproof		
fluency		fodder		foolscap		
fluent		foe		foot		
fluently		fog		football		
fluffy		foggy		footboard		
fluid		foil		foothold		
fluke		foist		footmark		
flung		fold		footnote		
fluorescent		folder		footpath		
fluoride		foliage		footprint		
flurry		folio		footstep		
flush		folk		footwear		
fluster		folklore		*for*		
flute		follow		forage		
flutter		follower		foray		
flux		folly		forbade forbad		
fly		fond		forbear		
flyer flier		fondle		forbearance		
flyover		fondly		forbid		
flyweight		food		forbidden		
flywheel		fool		force		
foal		foolhardy		forceful		
foam		foolish		forcefully		
fob		foolishly		forceps		

74

forces		forestry		format	
forcibly		foretell		formation	
ford		forever		formative	
fore		forewarn		former	
foreboding		foreword		formerly	
forecast		forfeit		formidable	
foreclose		forfeiture		formula	
foreclosure		forge		formulate	
forego		forger		forsake	
foregone		forgery		fort	
forehead		forget		forth	
foreign		forgetful		forthcoming	
foreigner		forgive		forthright	
foreman		forgiveness		forthwith	
foremost		forgo		fortieth	40. or
forensic		forgot		fortify	
forerunner		forgotten		fortitude	
foresee		fork		fortnight	
foreseen		forlorn		fortress	
foreshadow		forlornly		fortuitous	
foreshore		form		fortunate	
foreshorten		formal		fortunately	
forest		formality		fortune	
forestall		formally		forty	40. or

75

forum

fracture

fray

forward

fragile

freak

fossil

fragment

free

foster

fragmentary

freedom

fought

fragrance

freehold

foul

fragrant

freelance

foully

frail

freely

found

frailty

freer

foundation

frame

freest

founder

framer

freewill

foundry

franc

freeze

fount

franchise

freight

fountain

frank

freighter

four

frankly

frenzy

foursome

frankness

frequency

four-square

frantic

frequent

fourteen

frantically

frequently

fourteenth

fraternal

fresh

fourth

fraternally

freshen

fowl

fraternity

fresher

fox

fraud

freshest

fracas

fraudulent

freshly

fraction

fraudulently

fret

fractious

fraught

fretful

fretwork		frock		fruition		
friar		frog		fruitless		
friction		frolic		fruitlessly		
Friday		from		frump		
fried		front		frustrate		
friend		frontage		frustration		
friendless		frontal		fry		
friendliness		frontier		fudge		
friendly		frontispiece		fuel		
friendship		frost		fugitive		
frieze		frostbite		fulfil		
				fulfill		
frigate		frosty		fulfilment		
				fulfillment		
fright		froth		full		
frighten		frown		full-length		
frightful		froze		fullness		
				fulness		
frightfully		frozen		full-stop		
frigid		frugal		fully		
frill		frugality		fulminate		
fringe		frugally		fumble		
frisk		fruit		fume		
fritter		fruiterer		fumigate		
frivolity		fruitful		fun		
frivolous		fruitfully		function		
fro		fruitfulness		functional		

functionary		furl		furthest		
fund		furlong		furtive		
fundamen- tally		furlough		furtively		
fund-raising		furnace		fury		
funeral		furnish		fuse		
funereal		furnisher		fusion		
fungus		furniture		fuss		
funnel		furore		fussy		
funnier		furrier		futile		
funniest		furrow		futility		
funny		further		future		
fur		furtherance		futurist		
furious		furthermore		futuristic		
furiously		furthermost		fuzzy		

G

gable		galore		garish	
gadget		galosh golosh		garland	
Gaelic		galvanize		garment	
gag		gambit		garnish	
gaiety		gamble		garret	
gaily		gambol		garrison	
gain		game		garrulous	
gainful		gammon		garter	
gainfully		gamut		gas	
gainsay		gang		gas-cooker	
gait		gangrene		gash	
gala		gangster		gasket	
galaxy		gangway		gasoline gasolene	
gale		gaol		gasp	
gall		gap		gas-stove	
gallant		gape		gastric	
gallantly		garage		gate	
gallantry		garb		gate-house	
gallery		garbage		gatepost	
galley		garbled		gather	
gallon		garden		gauche	
gallop		gardener		gaudy	
gallows		gargle		gauge gage	

gaunt		generously		geometry	
gauntlet		genesis		geriatrics	
gauze		genetics		germ	
gave		genial		germinate	
gavotte		geniality		gestation	
gay		genially		gesticulate	
gaze		genius		gesture	
gazette		genteel		get	
gear		Gentile		geyser	
geese		gentility		ghastly	
gelatine		gentle		ghost	
gem		*gentleman*		ghoulish	
gender		*gentlemanly*		giant	
genealogy		*gentlemen*		gibe	
general		gentleness		giddy	
generality		gently		gift	
generalization		genuine		gigantic	
generalize		genuinely		gild	
generally		geographical		gill (of a fish)	
generate		geographically		gill (a measure)	
generation		geography		gilt	
generator		geological		gilt-edged	
generosity		geologist		gimmick	
generous		geology		gin	

80

ginger		gland		glorify	
gingerly		glandular		glorious	
gipsy gypsy		glare		gloriously	
gird		glass		glory	
girder		glassful		gloss	
girdle		glassware		glossary	
girl		glassy		glossier	
girlish		glaze		glossiest	
girlishly		gleam		glossy	
giro		glean		glove	
girth		glee		glow	
gist		glib		glucose	
give		glibly		glue	
given		glide		glum	
glacier		glimmer		glumly	
glad		glimpse		glut	
gladden		glint		glutinous	
glade		glitter		glutton	
gladly		gloaming		gluttonous	
gladness		gloat		gluttonously	
glamorous		globe		glycerin(e)	
glamorously		gloom		gnarled	
glamour		gloomily		gnash	
glance		gloomy		gnaw	

go	gooseberry	grade
goad	gorge	gradient
go-ahead	gorgeous	gradual
goal	gorgeously	gradually
goat	gorgonzola	graduate
go-between	gospel	graduation
goblet	gossip	graft
God	got	grain
godly	gouge	grammar
goes	gourmet	grammatical
gold	gout	grammatically
golden	govern	gramme
golf	government	granary
gone	govern-mental	grand
gong	governor	grandchild
good	governorship	grand-daughter
good-bye	gown	grandeur
good-humoured	grab	grandfather
good-looking	grace	grandmother
good-natured	graceful	grandparent
goodness	gracefully	grandson
good-night	gracious	granite
goodwill	graciously	grant
goose	gradation	grantor

82

granular		gravitation		grieve	
granulate		gravity		grievous	
grape		gravy		grievously	
graph		graze		grill grille	
graphic		grease		grim	
graphically		greasy		grimace	
graphite		great		grime	
grapple		greater		grimly	
grasp		greatest		grin	
grass		greatly		grind	
grassy		greatness		grip	
grate		greed		gripe	
grateful		greedily		grisly	
gratefully		greedy		grist	
gratification		green		gristle	
gratify		greengrocer		grit	
gratis		greenhouse		groan	
gratitude		greet		grocer	
gratuity		gregarious		grocery	
grave		grenade		groom	
gravedigger		grew		groove	
gravel		grey gray		grope	
gravely		grief		gross	
graven		grievance		grotesque	

83

ground

guarantee

gull

groundless

guarantor

gullet

groundwork

guard

gullible

group

guardian

gulp

grove

guess

gum

grovel

guesswork

gumption

grow

guest

gun

grower

guesthouse

gunfire

growl

guidance

gunpowder

grown

guide

gurgle

growth

guideline

gush

grub

guild

gust

grudge

guilder

gusto

grudgingly

guile

gut

gruelling

guilt

gutter

gruesome

guiltily

guy

gruff

guilty

guzzle

gruffly

guise

gymnasium

grumble

guitar

gymnastics

grumpy

gulden

gyrate

grunt

gulf

gyroscope

H

habilitate	hallow	hand-out	
habit	Halloween	handsome	
habitation	halo	handsomely	
habitual	halt	handwork	
habitually	halter	handwriting	
hack	halve	handy	
hackle	ham	hang	
hackneyed	hamlet	hangar	
had	hammer	hanger	
haddock	hammock	hanker	
haemorrhage hemorrhage	hamper	haphazard	
hag	hamstrung	hapless	
haggard	hand	happen	
haggis	handbag	happier	
haggle	handbook	happiest	
hail	handcuff	happiness	
hair	handful	happy	
halcyon	handicap	harangue	
hale	handicraft	harass	
half-caste	handily	harbour harbor	
half-hearted	handiwork	hard	
hall	handkerchief	hard-earned	
hallmark	handle	harden	

harder		harsh		hay
hardest		harshly		hazard
hard-hearted		harvest		hazardous
hardier		*has*		haze
hardiest		hash		hazily
hardly		haste		haziness
hardness		hasten		hazy
hardship		hastily		he
hardware		hasty		head
hardwood		hat		headache
hardy		hatch		headland
hare		hatchet		headlight
hark		hate		headline
harm		hateful		headlong
harmful		hatefully		headmaster
harmfully		hatred		headmistress
harmless		haughtily		headquarters
harmonious		haughty		headstrong
harmoniously		haul		headway
harmonize		haunt		heal
harmony		*have*		health
harness		haven		healthful
harp		havoc		healthier
harrow		hawk		healthiest

86

healthy		heavenly		helmet	
heap		heavier		help	
hear		heaviest		helpful	
heard		heavily		helpfully	
hearer		heaviness		helpless	
hearsay		heavy		helplessly	
hearse		heavyweight		helplessness	
heart		Hebrew		helter-skelter	
heartbroken		heckle		hem	
heartfelt		hectic		hemisphere	
hearth		hectically		hemp	
heartily		hedge		hen	
heartless		heed		hence	
heartlessly		heedful		henceforth	
heartrending		heedless		hence-forward	
hearty		heel		her	
heat		height		herald	
heater		heir		heraldry	
heath		heiress		herb	
heathen		heirloom		herbaceous	
heather		held		herbalist	
heatwave		hell		herd	
heave		hello		here	
heaven		helm		hereabouts	

87

hereafter		hesitant		highland
hereby		hesitantly		highlight
hereditary		hesitate		highly
heredity		hesitation		high-minded
herein		heterogeneous		highness
herinafter		hew		high-pitched
hereof		hewn		highroad
hereon		hexagon		high-spirited
hereto		heyday		highway
heretofore		hiatus		hike
herewith		hibernation		hilarious
heritage		hid		hilarity
hermetic		hidden		hill
hermetically		hide		hillside
hermit		hidebound		hilt
hero		hideous		him
heroic		hierarchy		himself
heroically		high		hinder
heroine		highbrow		hindrance
heroism		high-class		Hindu
				Hindoo
herring		higher		hinge
hers		highest		hint
herself		high-handed		hip
hesitancy		high-heeled		hire

his		hoist		honesty	
hiss		hold		honey	
historian		holder		honeymoon	
historic		hold-up		honorary	
historical		hole		honour honor	
historically		holiday		honourable honorable	
history		holiness		honourably honorably	
hit		hollow		hood	
hitch		holly		hoodwink	
hither		holocaust		hoof	
hither*to*		holy		hook	
hive		homage		hoop	
hoard		home		hoot	
hoarder		homecoming		hop	
hoarse		homeless		hope	
hoarsely		homely		hopeful	
hoax		homesick		hopefully	
hobble		homestead		hopefulness	
hobby		homeward		hopeless	
hobnob		homicide		hopelessly	
hockey		homily		hopelessness	
hod		homogeneous		horizon	
hoe		honest		horizontal	
hog		honestly		horizontally	

horn		hostel		*how*		
hornet		hostess		however		
horrible		hostile		howl		
horribly		hostility		howsoever		
horrid		hot		hub		
horrific		hotchpotch		huckleberry		
horrify		hotel		huckster		
horror		hothouse		huddle		
horse		hotter		hue		
horseback		hottest		huff		
horsehair		hound		hug		
horseman		*hour*		huge		
horse-power		*hourly*		hugely		
horse-racing		house		hulk		
horticulture		household		hull		
hose		householder		hum		
hosiery		housekeeper		human		
hospitable		housekeeping		humane		
hospitably		housewarming		humanely		
hospital		housewife		humanitarian		
hospitality		housework		humanity		
hospitalization		hovel		humanly		
host		hover		humble		
hostage		hovercraft		humbly		

90

humbug	hunter	hydro-dynamics
humid	hurdle	hydro-electric
humidifier	hurl	hydrogen
humidity	hurrah	hygiene
humiliate	hurricane	hygienic
humiliation	hurry	hygienically
humility	hurt	hymn
humorist	hurtful	hyphen
humorous	husband	hypnotism
humorously	husbandry	hypocrisy
humour humor	hush	hypocrite
hump	husk	hypocritical
hunch	husky	hypothesis
hundred	hustings	hypothetic
hundredth	hustle	hypothetical
hundredweight	hustler	hypothetically
hung	hut	hysteria
hunger	hybrid	hysterical
hungry	hydraulic	hysterically
hunt	hydraulically	hysterics

I

I		idle		illogical	
ice		idly		illogically	
iceberg		idolatry		ill-timed	
icebox		idolize		illuminate	
ice-cream		idyllic		illumination	
icicle		if		illumine	
icy		ignite		ill-used	
idea		ignition		illusion	
ideal		ignominious		illusory	
idealism		ignoramus		illustrate	
idealist		ignorance		illustration	
idealistic		ignorant		illustrative	
idealistically		ignorantly		illustrator	
ideally		ignore		illustrious	
identical		ill		ill-will	
identification		illegal		image	
identify		illegally		imagery	
identity		illegible		imaginary	
idiocy		illegitimate		imagination	
idiom		illicit		imaginative	
idiosyncrasy		illiterate		imaginatively	
idiot		ill-natured		imagine	
idiotic		illness		imbecile	

92

imitate		immorality		impel	
imitation		immorally		impend	
immaculate		immortal		imperative	
immaterial		immortality		imperatively	
immature		immovable		imperceptible	
immeasurable		immune		imperfect	
immeasurably		immunity		imperfection	
immediate		imp		imperfectly	
immediately		impact		imperial	
immemorial		impair		imperialism	
immense		impart		imperialist	
immensely		impartial		imperishable	
immensity		impartiality		impersonal	
immerse		impartially		impersonation	
immersion		impassable		impertinence	
immigrant		impatience		impertinent	
immigration		impatient		impertinently	
imminent		impatiently		imperturbable	
immobile		impeach		impervious	
immoderate		impeccable		impetuous	
immoderately		impeccably		impetuously	
immodest		impecunious		impetus	
immodestly		impede		impinge	
immoral		impediment		implacable	

93

implacably	impoverish	imprudent
implausible	impracticable	imprudently
implement	impractical	impudence
implemen- tation	impregnable	impudent
implicate	impregnate	impulse
implication	impress	impulsive
implicit	impression	impulsively
implicitly	impressionable	impure
implore	impressive	impurity
imply	impressively	*in*
impolite	imprint	inability
impolitely	imprison	inaccessible
import	imprisonment	inaccuracy
importance	improbability	inaccurate
important	improbable	inaccurately
importer	impromptu	inactive
impose	improper	inactivity
imposition	improperly	inadequate
impossibility	improve	inadequately
impossible	improvement	inanimate
imposter	improvident	inapplicable
impotence	improvisation	inappropriate
impotent	improvise	inappropriately
impound	imprudence	inarticulate

94

*inas*much		incidental		inconceivable	
inattention		incidentally		inconclusive	
inattentive		incinerate		inconclusively	
inattentively		incinerator		inconsiderable	
inaudible		incision		inconsiderate	
inaugural		incite		inconsistency	
inaugurate		incitement		inconsistent	
inauguration		incivility		inconsistently	
inauspicious		inclination		inconspicuous	
incalculable		include		incontrovertible	
incapability		inclusion		inconvenience	
incapable		inclusive		inconvenient	
incapacitate		incognito		inconveniently	
incapacity		incoherent		incorporate	
incarcerate		incoherently		incorporation	
incendiary		income		incorrect	
incense		income-tax		incorrectly	
incentive		incomparable		incorruptible	
inception		incompatibility		increase	
incessant		incompatible		increasingly	
incessantly		incompetence		incredible	
inch		incompetent		incredulous	
incidence		incomplete		increment	
incident		incompre-hensible		incriminate	

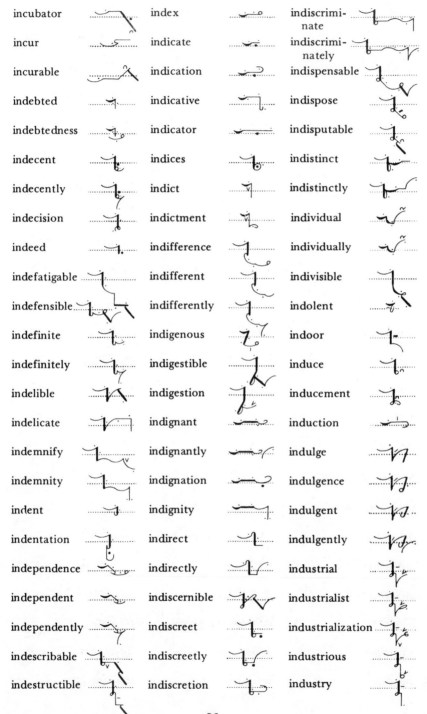

incubator	index	indiscriminate
incur	indicate	indiscriminately
incurable	indication	indispensable
indebted	indicative	indispose
indebtedness	indicator	indisputable
indecent	indices	indistinct
indecently	indict	indistinctly
indecision	indictment	individual
indeed	indifference	individually
indefatigable	indifferent	indivisible
indefensible	indifferently	indolent
indefinite	indigenous	indoor
indefinitely	indigestible	induce
indelible	indigestion	inducement
indelicate	indignant	induction
indemnify	indignantly	indulge
indemnity	indignation	indulgence
indent	indignity	indulgent
indentation	indirect	indulgently
independence	indirectly	industrial
independent	indiscernible	industrialist
independently	indiscreet	industrialization
indescribable	indiscreetly	industrious
indestructible	indiscretion	industry

inedible		infancy		infirmity	
inefficiency		infant		inflame	
inefficient		infantile		inflammable	
inefficiently		infantry		inflammation	
inelegant		infatuate		inflate	
inept		infatuation		inflation	
ineptitude		infect		inflexible	
inequality		infection		inflict	
inert		infectious		infliction	
inertia		infer		*influence*	
inescapable		inference		*influential*	
inestimable		inferior		*influentially*	
inevitable		inferiority		influenza	
inexact		infernal		influx	
inexcusable		inferno		inform	
inexhaustible		infest		informal	
inexpensive		infidelity		informality	
inexperience		infiltrate		informally	
inexpert		infinite		informant	
inexplicable		infinitely		*information*	
inexpressible		infinitive		informative	
infallible		infinity		informer	
infamous		infirm		infrequent	
infamy		infirmary		infrequently	

infringe	initial	innocent
infringement	initially	innocently
infuriate	initiate	innovation
infuse	initiation	innumerable
ingenious	initiative	inoculate
ingenuity	inject	inopportune
ingot	injection	inopportunely
ingrain	injunction	inorganic
ingratiate	injure	input
ingratitude	injurious	inquest
ingredient	injury	inquisitive
inhabit	injustice	inquisitively
inhabitant	ink	inroad
inhale	inlaid	insane
inhere	inland	insanitary
inherent	inlet	insanity
inherit	inmate	insatiable
inheritance	inmost	inscribe
inheritor	inn	inscriber
inhibition	innate	inscription
inhospitable	innately	inscrutable
inhuman	inner	insect
inhumanly	innermost	insecticide
iniquity	innocence	insecure

insecurely		insistently		instigator	
insecurity		insolence		instil(l)	
insemination		insolent		instinct	or
insensible		insolently		instinctive	or
insensitive		insoluble		instinctively	or
inseparable		insolvent		institute	
insert		insomnia		institution	
insertion		inspect		instruct	
inset		inspection		instruction	
inside		inspector		instructive	
insight		inspiration		instructor	
insignia		inspire		instrument	
insignificance		instability		instrumental	
insignificant		install		insubordination	
insignificantly		installation		insubstantial	
insincere		instalment installment		insufferable	
insincerely		instance		insufficient	
insincerity		instant		insufficiently	
insinuate		instantaneous		insular	
insinuation		instantly		insulate	
insipid		instead		insulation	
insist		instep		insulator	
insistence		instigate		insulin	
insistent		instigation		insult	

99

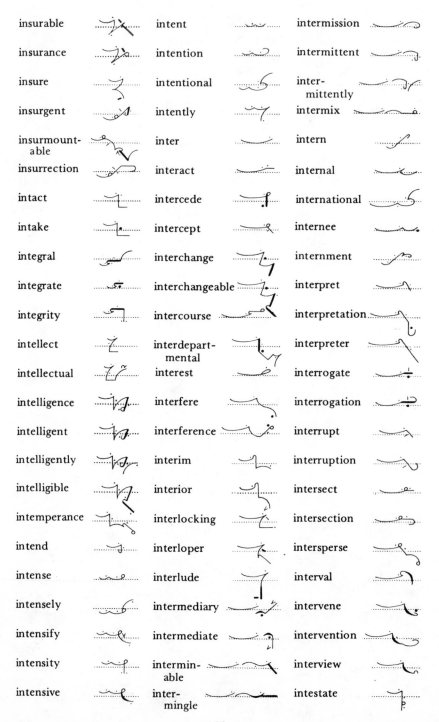

insurable	intent	intermission
insurance	intention	intermittent
insure	intentional	inter-mittently
insurgent	intently	intermix
insurmount-able	inter	intern
insurrection	interact	internal
intact	intercede	international
intake	intercept	internee
integral	interchange	internment
integrate	interchangeable	interpret
integrity	intercourse	interpretation
intellect	interdepart-mental	interpreter
intellectual	interest	interrogate
intelligence	interfere	interrogation
intelligent	interference	interrupt
intelligently	interim	interruption
intelligible	interior	intersect
intemperance	interlocking	intersection
intend	interloper	intersperse
intense	interlude	interval
intensely	intermediary	intervene
intensify	intermediate	intervention
intensity	intermin-able	interview
intensive	inter-mingle	intestate

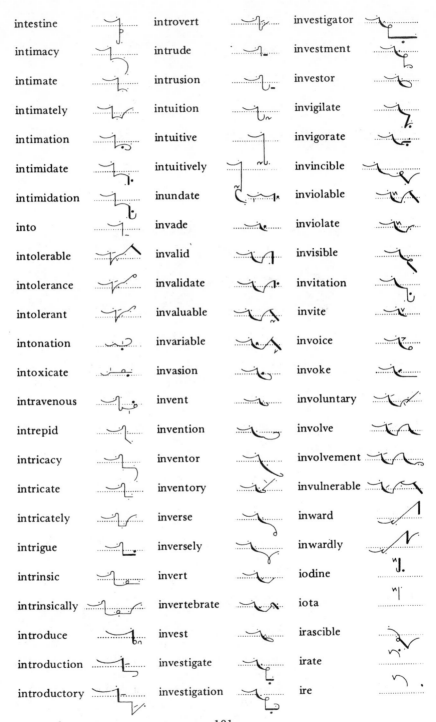

intestine	introvert	investigator
intimacy	intrude	investment
intimate	intrusion	investor
intimately	intuition	invigilate
intimation	intuitive	invigorate
intimidate	intuitively	invincible
intimidation	inundate	inviolable
into	invade	inviolate
intolerable	invalid	invisible
intolerance	invalidate	invitation
intolerant	invaluable	invite
intonation	invariable	invoice
intoxicate	invasion	invoke
intravenous	invent	involuntary
intrepid	invention	involve
intricacy	inventor	involvement
intricate	inventory	invulnerable
intricately	inverse	inward
intrigue	inversely	inwardly
intrinsic	invert	iodine
intrinsically	invertebrate	iota
introduce	invest	irascible
introduction	investigate	irate
introductory	investigation	ire

iris		irrepressible	*is*	
irksome		irreproachable	island	
iron		irresistible	isle	
ironical		irresolute	isolate	
ironmonger		irrespective	isolation	
irony		irrespectively	issue	
irrational		irresponsibility	isthmus	
irreconcilable		irresponsible	*it*	
irrecoverable		irrespons- ibly	italic	
irredeemable		irretrievable	italicize	
irrefutable		irreverent	itch	
irregular		irreverently	item	
irregularity		irrevocable	iterate	
irregularly		irrigate	itinerant	
irrelevance		irrigation	itinerary	
irrelevant		irritable	its	
irrelevantly		irritant	itself	
irremovable		irritate	ivory	
irreparable		irritation	ivy	

102

jab	jealousy	jigsaw
jack	jeans	jingle
jacket	jeer	jitters
jade	jelly	job
jag	jeopardize	jobber
jagged	jeopardy	jobbing
jaguar	jerk	jockey
jail	jerry-built	jocose
jailbird	jersey	jocular
jailer jailor	jest	jocularly
jam	jet	jog
jamboree	jet-propelled	join
jangle	jetsam	joiner
janitor	jettison	joinery
January	jetty	joint
jar	Jew	jointed
jargon	jewel	jointly
jaundice	jeweller jeweler	joint-stock
jaunt	jewellery jewelry	joist
jaunty	Jewess	joke
jauntily	Jewish	jollity
jaw	jibe	jolly
jealous	jig	jolt

jostle	judder	jungle
jot	judge	junior
journal	judgment	junk
	judgement	
journalism	judicial	junta
journalist	judicially	juridical
journalistic	judicious	jurisdiction
journalize	judiciously	jurisprudence
journey	judo	jurist
jovial	jug	juror
jovially	juggle	jury
jowl	juggler	just
joy	jugular	justice
joyful	juice	justifiable
joyfully	July	justifiably
joyous	jumble	justification
joyously	jumbo	justify
jubilant	jump	justly
jubilantly	jumper	jut
jubilation	junction *or*	jute
jubilee	juncture *or*	juvenile
Judaism	June	juxtaposition

104

K

kaleidoscope	kick	kindred
kangaroo	kicker	kine
keel	kid	king
keen	kidnap	kingdom
keener	kidnapper / kidnaper	king-pin
keenest	kidney	king-post
keenly	kill	kingship
keep	kiln	kink
keeper	kilogram	kinsfolk
keepsake	kilometre / kilometer	kinship
keg	kilowatt	kinsman
kennel	kilowatt-*hour*	kiss
kept	kilt	kit
kerb	kin	kitchen
kernel	kind	kite
kerosene	kinder	kitten
kettle	kindergarten	kitty
key	kindest	klaxon
keyboard	kind-hearted	knack
keyhole	kind-heartedly	knave
keynote	kindle	knead
keypunch	kindly	knee
khaki	kindness	kneel

knell	knock	knowingly
knelt	knocker	knowledge
knew	knock-kneed	knowledgeable
knife	knock-out	known
knife-edge	knoll	knuckle
knight	knot	kopeck
		kopek
knit	knotty	kosher
knives	know	kraal
knob	know-how	kudos

L

label	lament	laryngitis
laboratory	lamentable	lash
laborious	laminated	lass
labour labor	lamp	last
labourer laborer	lance	lastly
lace	land	latch
lacerate	landlord	late
lack	landowner	lat(e)ish
lacquer lacker	landscape	lately
lad	lane	latent
ladder	language	later
laden	languid	lateral
ladle	lantern	latest
lady	lap	lathe
lag	lapel	lather
lager	lapse	Latin
laid	larch	latitude
lain	lard	latter
lair	larder	latterly
laity	*large*	laud
lake	*largely*	laudable
lamb	*larger*	laugh
lame	*largest*	laughter

launch	lazy	least
laundry	lead (metal)	leather
laurel	lead	leave
lavatory	leaden	lecture
lavender	leader	lecturer
lavish	leadership	led
lavishly	leaf	ledge
law	leaflet	ledger
lawful	leafy	leek
lawfully	league	leeway
lawless	leak	left
lawn	leakage	lefthanded
lawsuit	leaky	leg
lawyer	lean	legacy
lax	leant	legal
laxative	leap	legality
lay	leapt	legalize
layer	learn	legally
layman	learnèd	legend
layout	learner	legendary
laze	learnt	legibility
laziest	lease	legible
lazily	leasehold	legion
laziness	leash	legislate

legislation	lest	library
legislative	let	licence / license
legislator	lethal	licencee / licensee
legislature	lethargy	lick
legitimacy	letter	lid
legitimate	lettuce	lie
leisure	level	lien
leisurely	lever	lieu
lemon	leverage	lieutenant
lemonade	levity	life
lend	levy	lifetime
lender	liability	lift
length	liable	ligature
lengthen	liaison	light
lengthy	liar	lightening
lenient	libel	lighter
leniently	libellous / libelous	lightest
lens	liberal	lighthearted
lent	liberality	lighthouse
less	liberally	lightly
lessen	liberate	lightning
lesser	liberation	like
lesson	liberty	likeable / likable
lessor	librarian	likelihood

likely		lint		litigate	
liken		lion		litigation	
likeness		lioness		litre	
likewise		lip		litter	
lilt		liquefy		little	
limb		liqueur		live, *v*	
limbless		liquid		live, *adj*	
lime		liquidate		liveable livable	
limit		liquidation		livelihood	
limitation		liquidator		lively	
limitless		liquor		liver	
limp		lisp		livery	
limpid		list		livestock	
line		listen		livid	
lineage		listener		lizard	
lineal		listless .		load	
linen		lit		loaf	
liner		literal		loafer	
linger		literally		loam	
linguist		literary		loan	
liniment		literate		loath loth	
link		literature		loathe	
linoleum		lithe		loathsome	
linseed		lithography		loaves	

110

lob		loiter		loot	
lobby		loll		lop	
local		lone		loquacious	
locality		loneliness		lord	
localize		lonely		lore	
locally		lonesome		lorry	
locate		long		lose	
location		longer		loser	
loch lock		longest		loss	
locker		longhand		lot	
locket		longitude		lotion	
locomotion		longitudinal		lottery	
locomotive		long-lived		lotus	
locum		longstanding		loud	
lodge		long-suffering		louder	
loft		long-term		loudest	
loftily		look		lounge	
lofty		lookout		lout	
log		loom		lovable	
loggerheads		loop		love	
logic		loophole		loveless	
logical		loose		loveliness	
logically		loosely		lovely	
loin		loosen		lover	

lovingly		ludicrous	lure
low		lug	lurid
lower, *adj*		luggage	lurk
lower, *v*		lugubrious	luscious
lowest		lukewarm	lush
lowland		lull	lust
lowly		lullaby	lustily
loyal		lumbago	lustre
			luster
loyalty		lumber	lusty
lozenge		luminous	lute
lubricant		lump	luxuriance
lubricate		lunacy	luxuriant
lubrication		lunar	luxuriate
lucid		lunatic	luxurious
luck		lunch	luxury
luckier		luncheon	lymph
luckless		lung	lynch
lucky		lunge	lyric
lucrative		lurch	lyrical

M

Ma	magnificence	make
mace	magnificent	maker
machine	magnificently	makeshift
machinery	magnify	make-up
machinist	magnitude	malady
mad	mahogany	malaria
madam madame	maid	male
made	maiden	malevolent
madly	mail	malice
madman	maim	malicious
madness	main	maliciously
magazine	mainland	malign
magic	mainly	malignant
magician	mainspring	malleable
magistrate	mainstay	mallet
magnanimous	maintain	malt
magnate	maintenance	maltreat
magnesium	maisonette	Mama Mamma
magnet	maize	mammal
magnetic	majestic	mammoth
magnetism	majesty	man
magnetize	major	manacle
magneto	majority	manage

113

manageable	mankind	margin
management	manly	marine
manager	manner	mariner
manageress	manoeuvre manoeuver	marital
managerial	manor	maritime
mandate	manpower	mark
mandatory	mansion	marker
mane	manslaughter	market
manfully ... or ...	mantel	marketable
manger	mantle	marketplace
mangle	manual	maroon
manhandle	manufacture	marriage
manhole	manufacturer	marrow
manhood	manure	marry
mania	manuscript	marsh
maniac	many	marshal
manicure	map	martial
manifest	maple	martyr
manifestation	mar	martyrdom
manifesto	marauder	marvel
manifold	marble	marvellous marvelous
manila	March (march)	Marxist
manipulate	mare	mascot
manipulation	margarine	masculine

114

mash		mathematical		meadow	
mason		mathematically		meagre meager	
masonic		mathematician		meal	
masonry		mathematics		mealtime	
masquerade		matinee		mean	
mass		matriculate		meander	
massacre		matriculation		meaningless	
massage		matrimonial		meant	
massive		matrimony		meantime	
mast		matron		meanwhile	
master		matter		measurable	
masterful		mattress		measure	
masterly		mature		measurement	
masterpiece		maturity		meat	
mastery		maul		mechanic	
mat		mauve		mechanical	
match		maxim		mechanically	
matchless		maximum		mechanism	
mate		May (may)		mechanization	
material		maybe		mechanize	
materialistic		mayonnaise		medal meddle	
materialize		mayor		media	
maternal		maze		medi(a)eval	
maternity		me		medial	

115

mediate	memoir	merciless
mediation	memorable	mercy
medical	memoranda	mere
medicated	memoran-dum	merely
medicinal	memorial	merge
medicine	memorize	merger
mediocre	memory	merit
mediocrity	men	merriment
meditate	menace	merry
meditation	mend	mesh
medium	menfolk	mesmerize
medley	menial	mess
meek	meningitis	message
meet	mental	messenger
melancholy	mentality	Messrs
mellow	mention	met
melodious	mentor	metal
melody	menu	metamor-phosis
melon	mercantile	metaphor
melt	mercenary	metaphorically
member	merchandise	mete
membership	merchant	meteor
membrane	merciful	meteoric
memento	mercifully	meteorology

116

metre		middle		mil(e)age	
meter		middle-aged		milestone	
method		middle-class		militant	
methodical		middleman		military	
Methodist		midge		militate	
methylated		midget		militia	
meticulous		midnight	*or*	milk	
metric		midst		milkman	
metropolis		midsummer		milky	
metropolitan		midway		mill	
mettle		midwestern		miller	
mice		midwife		millimetre	
Michaelmas		midwinter		milliner	
microbe		mien		millinery	
microbiology		might		million	
microcosm		mighty		millionaire	
microfilm		migraine		millpond	
micrometer		migrant		mime	
micronometer		migrate		mimic	
microphone		migratory		mince	
microscope		mild		mincemeat	
microscopic		mildew		mind	
mid		mildly		mindful	
midday		mile		mine	

117

minefield	mirth	mislaid
miner	mirthful	mislead
mineral	misappre- hension	mismanage
mingle	misappro- priation	misplace
miniature	misbehave	misprint
minimal	misbehaviour misbehavior	mis- pronounce
minimize	miscellaneous	misquote
minimum	mischief	misrepresent
minister	mischievous	misrepresen tation
ministerial	misconceive	miss
ministry	misconception	missile
minor	misconduct	mission
minority	misconstrue	missionary
minster	miscreant	missive
minstrel	misdemeanour misdemeanor	misspell
mint	misdirect	misstatement
minus	misery	mist
minute, *n & v*	misfit	mistake
minute, *adj*	misfortune	mistaken
miracle	misgiving	mistook
miraculous	misguided	mistress
mirage	mishap	mistrust
mire	misinform	misty
mirror	misinterpret	misunderstand

misunderstood	modern	money
misuse, *v & n*	modernization	mongrel
mite	modernize	monitor
mitigate	modest	monk
mitigation	modesty	monkey
mitre	modification	monogram
mix	modify	monograph
mixer	modulate	monolithic
mixture	Mohammedan	monoplane
mnemonic	moist	monopolize
moan	moisten	monopoly
moat	moisture	monosyllabic
mob	mole	monotonous
mobile	molecule	monotony
mobility	molest	Monotype
mobilization	molestation	monsoon
mock	molten	monster
mockery	momentarily	monstrosity
mode	momentary	monstrous
model	momentous	month
moderate, *n & adj*	monarch	monthly
moderate, *v*	monastery	monument
moderately	Monday	monumental
moderation	monetary	monumentally

mood	mortal	motor-car
moodily	mortality	motor-coach
moody	mortar	motor-cycle
moon	mortgage	motorist
moonlight	mortgagee	motorway
moonshine	mortgager mortgagor	mottled
moor	mortification	motto
moorland	mortify	mould mold
mop	moss	mouldy moldy
moped, *n*	most	moult
moral	mostly	mound
morale	motel	mount
moralist	moth	mountain
morality	mother	mountaineer
morbid	motherhood	mountainous
more	mother-*in*-law	mourn
*more*over	motherland	mourner
morgue	motif	mournful
morn	motion	mournfully
morning	motionless	mourning
moron	motivate	mouse
morrow	motive	moustache mustache
morse	motley	mouth
morsel	motor	mouthful

mouthpiece	multiply	musician
mov(e)able	multitude	must
move	Mum	mustard
movement	mumble	muster
mover	Mummy	musty
mow	munch	mute
mower	mundane	mutilate
mown	municipal	mutilation
Mr	municipality	mutiny
Mrs	mural	mutter
much	murder	mutton
muck	murderer	mutual
mud	murderess	muzzle
muddle	murderous	my
muddy	murky	myself
muff	murmur	mysterious
muffle	muscle	mystery
mule	muscular	mystic
mull	muse	mystify
multi-coloured	museum	mystique
multilateral	mushroom	myth
multiple	music	mythology
multiplication	musical	mythological

N

nag		national		navigate		
nail		nationality		navigation		
naive		nationalization		navigator		
naked		nationalize		navy		
name		nationally		nay		
nameless		nationwide		near		
namely		native		nearby		
napalm		nativity		nearer		
napkin		natural		nearest		
narcissus		naturalist		nearly		
narcotic		naturalization		neat		
narrate		naturalize		neatly		
narrative		naturally		nebulous		
narrator		nature		necessarily		
narrow		naught		necessary		
narrower		naughty		necessitate		
narrowest		nausea		necessitous		
narrowly		nauseating		necessity		
narrow-minded		nautical		neck		
nasal		naval		nectar		
nasty		nave		need		
natal		navel		needful		
nation		navigable		needle		

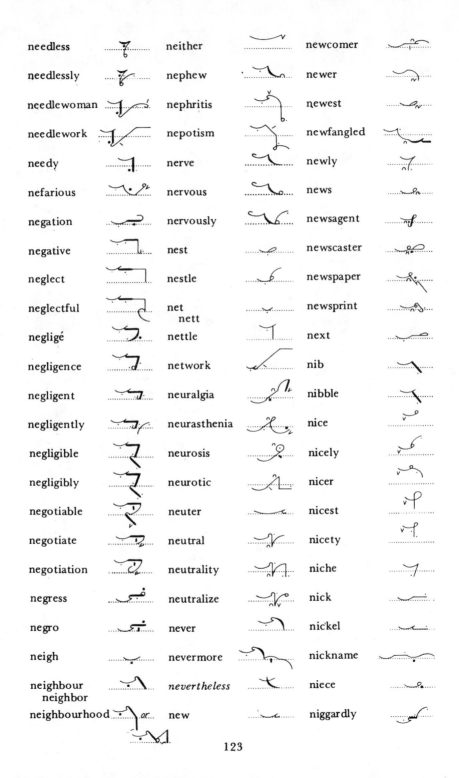

needless		neither		newcomer	
needlessly		nephew		newer	
needlewoman		nephritis		newest	
needlework		nepotism		newfangled	
needy		nerve		newly	
nefarious		nervous		news	
negation		nervously		newsagent	
negative		nest		newscaster	
neglect		nestle		newspaper	
neglectful		net		newsprint	
		nett			
negligé		nettle		next	
negligence		network		nib	
negligent		neuralgia		nibble	
negligently		neurasthenia		nice	
negligible		neurosis		nicely	
negligibly		neurotic		nicer	
negotiable		neuter		nicest	
negotiate		neutral		nicety	
negotiation		neutrality		niche	
negress		neutralize		nick	
negro		never		nickel	
neigh		nevermore		nickname	
neighbour neighbor		*nevertheless*		niece	
neighbourhood	*or*	new		niggardly	

123

nigh		noiseless		nook	
night		noiselessly		noon	
nightly		noisily		noonday	
nil		noisy		no-one	
nimble		nomad		noose	
nine		nomen-clature		nor	
nineteen		nominal		normal	
nineteenth		nominally		normally	
ninetieth		nominate		north	
ninety		nomination		north-east	
ninth		nominative		north-easter	
nip		nominee		north-eastern	
nipple		non-appearance		northerly	
nitrate		nonchalant		northern	
nitric		nonchalantly		northerner	
nitrogen		non-committal		northward	
no		non-committally		northwest	
nobility		non-conformist		north-westerly	
noble		nondescript		north-western	
nobly		none		nose	
nobody		nonentity		nostalgia	
nocturnal		nonplussed		nostril	
nod		nonsense		not	
noise		nonsensical		notability	

notable		novel		nullity	
notary		novelist		numb	
notation		novelty		number	
notch		November		numeral	
note		novice		numerate	
noteworthy		now		numerical	
nothing		nowadays		numerous	
notice		nowhere		nun	
noticeable		noxious		nuptials	
noticeably		nozzle		nurse	
notification		nuance		nursery	
notify		nub		nurture	
notion		nuclear		nut	
notoriety		nucleus		nutriment	
notorious		nude		nutrition	
notoriously		nudge		nutritious	
notwithstanding		nudity		nutritive	
nought		nugget		nutshell	
noun		nuisance		nuzzle	
nourish		null		nylon	
nourishment		nullify		nymph	

O

O, Oh	obligatory	obstetrics	
oaf	oblige	obstinacy	
oak	oblique	obstinate	
oar	obliterate	obstinately	
oasis	oblivion	obstreperous	
oath	oblivious	obstruct	
oatmeal	oblong	obstruction	
oats	obnoxious	obstructive	
obduracy	oboe	obtain	
obedience	obscene	obtainable	
obedient	obscure	obtrude	
obediently	obscurity	obtrusive	
obelisk	obsequious	obtrusively	
obese	observance	obtuse	
obesity	observant	obviate	
obey	observation	obvious	
obituary	observatory	obviously	
object	observe	occasion	
objection	observer	occasional	
objectionable	obsession	occident	
objective	obsolescence	occidental	
objectively	obsolete	occult	
obligation	obstacle	occupancy	

occupant	offence offense	oil-well
occupation	offend	oily
occupy	offender	ointment
occur	offensive	okay
occurrence	offensively	old
ocean	offer	older
o'clock	offhand	oldest
octagon	office	old-fashioned
octane	officer	olive
octave	official	omelette
octavo	officially	omen
October	officiate	ominous
oculist	officious	omission
odd	officiously	omit
oddity	offset	omnibus
oddment	offspring	omniscient
ode	often	omnivorous
odious	ogre	on
odorous	oil	once
odour odor	oil-field	one
of	oil-fired	onerous
off	oil-rig	oneself
offal	oilskin	one-sided
offchance	oil-tanker	one-way

onion		oppose		orb		
onlooker		opposite		orbit		
only		opposition		orchard		
onset		oppress		orchestra		
onslaught		oppression		orchid		
onward		oppressive		ordain		
ooze		oppressively		ordeal		
opaque		oppressor		order		
open		optic		orderly		
opener		optical		ordinance		
openly		optician		ordinarily		
opera		optimism		ordinary		
operate		optimistic		ordnance		
operatic		optimistically		ore		
operation		option		organ		
operative		optional		organic		
operator		opulent		organically		
operetta		or		organist		
opinion		oracle		organization		
opium		oral		organize		
opponent		orange		organizer		
opportune		oration		orgy		
opportunely		orator		orient		
opportunity		oratory		oriental		

128

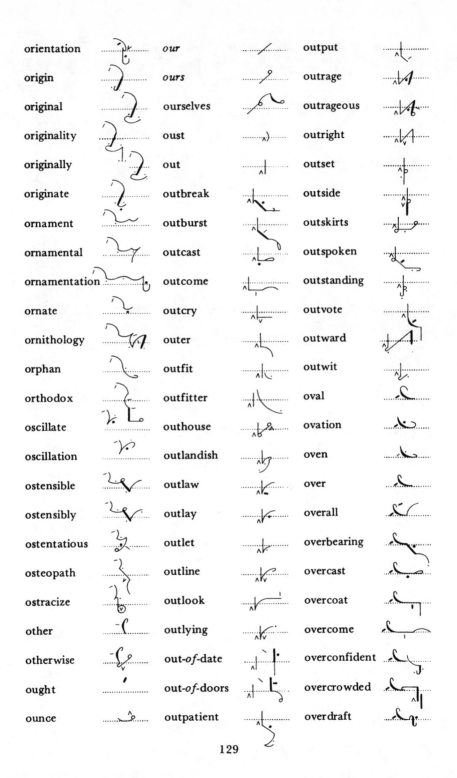

orientation	our	output
origin	ours	outrage
original	ourselves	outrageous
originality	oust	outright
originally	out	outset
originate	outbreak	outside
ornament	outburst	outskirts
ornamental	outcast	outspoken
ornamentation	outcome	outstanding
ornate	outcry	outvote
ornithology	outer	outward
orphan	outfit	outwit
orthodox	outfitter	oval
oscillate	outhouse	ovation
oscillation	outlandish	oven
ostensible	outlaw	over
ostensibly	outlay	overall
ostentatious	outlet	overbearing
osteopath	outline	overcast
ostracize	outlook	overcoat
other	outlying	overcome
otherwise	out-*of*-date	overconfident
ought	out-*of*-doors	overcrowded
ounce	outpatient	overdraft

overdrawn	overshadow	owl
overdue	oversight	own
overestimate	oversubscribe	owner
overflow	overt	ownership
overgrown	overtake	ox
overhand	overthrown	oxen
overhead	overtime	oxide
overhear	overtook	oxidize
overjoyed	overture	oxy-acetylene
over-rate	overwhelm	oxygen
over-rule	overwrought	oyster
overseas	*owe*	ozone

P

Pa		painlessly		pan	
pace		painstaking		panacea	
pacific		paint		pancreas	
pacifist		painter		pandemonium	
pacify		pair		pander	
pack		pal		pane	
package		palace		panegyric	
packer		palatable		panel	
packet		palate		pang	
pact		palatial		panic	
pad		pale		panoply	
paddle		pall		panorama	
paddock		palliative		pant	
padlock		pallid		pantomime	
pagan		pallor		pantry	
page		palm		Papa	
pageant		palpable		papacy	
pageantry		palpably		papal	
pail		palpitate		paper	
pain		palpitation		par	
painful		paltry		parable	
painfully		pamper		parachute	
painless		pamphlet		parade	

paradise		parish		partiality	
paradox		parishioner		partially	
paradoxical		parity		participant	
paradoxically		park		participate	
paraffin		parlance		participation	
paragon		parley		participle	
paragraph		parliament		particle	
parallel		parliamentary		particular	or
paralyse paralyze		parlour parlor		particularly	or
paralysis		parlous		partisan	
paramount		parochial		partition	
paraphrase		parody		partly	
parasite		parole		partner	
parcel		paroxysm		partnership	
parch		parquet		partook	
parchment		parrot		party	
pardon		parry		pass	
pare		parsimonious		passable	
parent		parsimoniously		passage	
parentage		parsnip		passenger	
parental		parson		passer-by	
parenthesis		part		passion	
parenthetical		partake		passionate	
parenthetically		partial		passionately	

132

passive		pathway		payee
passively		patience		payer
Passover		patient		payload
passport		patiently		paymaster
past		patriot		payment
paste		patriotic		payroll
pastel		patriotically		pea
pasteurize		patriotism		peace
pastime		patrol		peaceable
pastor		patron		peaceably
pastoral		patronage		peaceful
pastry		patronize		peacefully
pasture		patter		peach
pasty		pattern		peak
pat		paucity		peal
patch		pauper		peanut
patent		pause		pear
patentee		pave		pearl
patently		pavement		peasant
paternal		pavilion		peat
path		paw		pebble
pathetic		pawn		peck
pathetically		pay		pectoral
pathos		payable		peculation

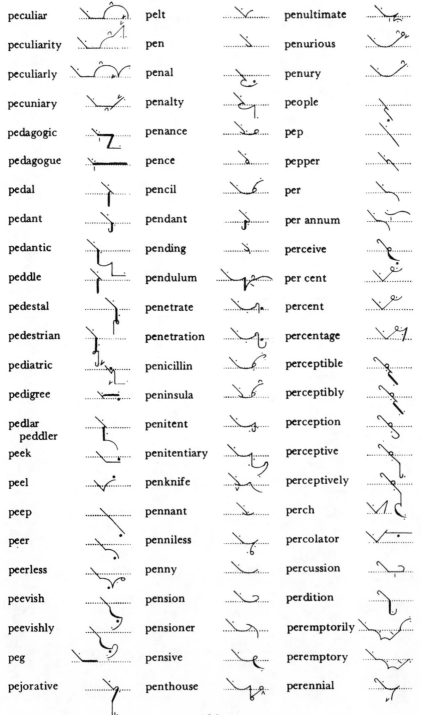

peculiar	pelt	penultimate
peculiarity	pen	penurious
peculiarly	penal	penury
pecuniary	penalty	people
pedagogic	penance	pep
pedagogue	pence	pepper
pedal	pencil	per
pedant	pendant	per annum
pedantic	pending	perceive
peddle	pendulum	per cent
pedestal	penetrate	percent
pedestrian	penetration	percentage
pediatric	penicillin	perceptible
pedigree	peninsula	perceptibly
pedlar peddler	penitent	perception
peek	penitentiary	perceptive
peel	penknife	perceptively
peep	pennant	perch
peer	penniless	percolator
peerless	penny	percussion
peevish	pension	perdition
peevishly	pensioner	peremptorily
peg	pensive	peremptory
pejorative	penthouse	perennial

134

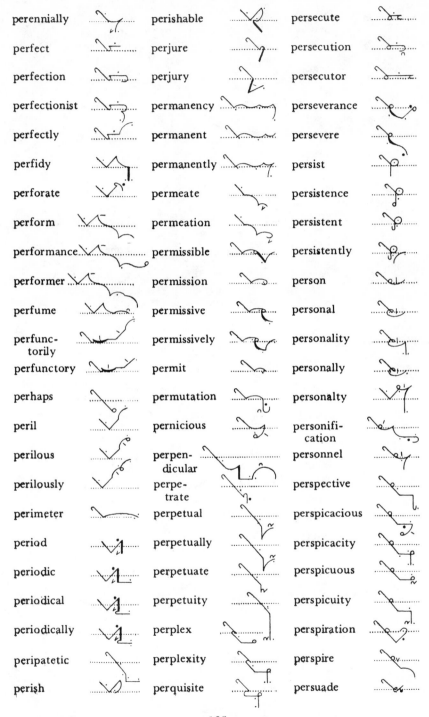

perennially	perishable	persecute
perfect	perjure	persecution
perfection	perjury	persecutor
perfectionist	permanency	perseverance
perfectly	permanent	persevere
perfidy	permanently	persist
perforate	permeate	persistence
perform	permeation	persistent
performance	permissible	persistently
performer	permission	person
perfume	permissive	personal
perfunc- torily	permissively	personality
perfunctory	permit	personally
perhaps	permutation	personalty
peril	pernicious	personifi- cation
perilous	perpen- dicular	personnel
perilously	perpe- trate	perspective
perimeter	perpetual	perspicacious
period	perpetually	perspicacity
periodic	perpetuate	perspicuous
periodical	perpetuity	perspicuity
periodically	perplex	perspiration
peripatetic	perplexity	perspire
perish	perquisite	persuade

135

persuasion	petitioner	philology
persuasive	petrify	philosopher
persuasively	petrol	philosophical
pertain	petroleum	philosophically
pertinacity	petticoat	philosophy
pertinent	pettifogging	phlebitis
perturb	petty	phlegmatic
perusal	petulant	phlegmatically
peruse	petulantly	phone
pervade	pewter	phonetic
perverse	phantom	phonetically
perversely	pharmacist	phoney
pervert	pharmacy	phosphorescent
peseta	phase	phosphorous
pessimism	phenomena	photo
pessimist	phenomenal	photocopy
pessimistic	phenomenally	photogenic
pest	phenomenon	photograph
pester	phial	photographer
pestilence	philanthropic	photographic
pestilent	philanthropist	photography
pet	philanthropy	photostat
petal	philharmonic	phrase
petition	philistine	physical

136

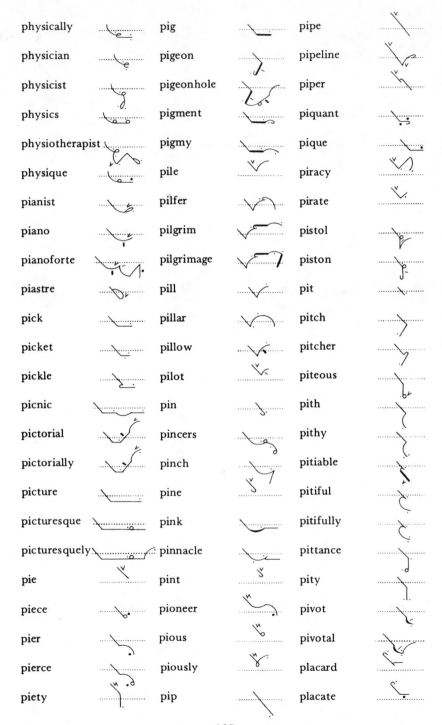

physically	pig	pipe	
physician	pigeon	pipeline	
physicist	pigeonhole	piper	
physics	pigment	piquant	
physiotherapist	pigmy	pique	
physique	pile	piracy	
pianist	pilfer	pirate	
piano	pilgrim	pistol	
pianoforte	pilgrimage	piston	
piastre	pill	pit	
pick	pillar	pitch	
picket	pillow	pitcher	
pickle	pilot	piteous	
picnic	pin	pith	
pictorial	pincers	pithy	
pictorially	pinch	pitiable	
picture	pine	pitiful	
picturesque	pink	pitifully	
picturesquely	pinnacle	pittance	
pie	pint	pity	
piece	pioneer	pivot	
pier	pious	pivotal	
pierce	piously	placard	
piety	pip	placate	

place		plastic		plebeian		
placid		plate		plebiscite		
plagiarism		plateau		pledge		
plague		platform		pleni- potentiary		
plaid		platinum		plenteous		
plain		platitude		plentiful		
plainer		plausibility		plentifully		
plainest		plausible		plenty		
plainly		play		pleurisy		
plaintiff		player		pliable		
plaintive		playful		pliers		
plait		playground		plight		
plan		playmate		plod		
plane		playroom		plot		
planet		plaything		plough plow		
planetarium		playwright		pluck		
plank		plea		plug		
plankton		plead		plum		
plant		pleasant		plumage		
plantation		pleasantly		plumb		
planter		please		plumber		
plaque		pleasurable		plume		
plaster		pleasure		plump		
plasterer		pleat		plunder		

plunge	pointlessly	pompous	
plunger	poise	pompously	
plural	poison	pond	
plus	poisonous	ponder	
plush	poke	ponderous	
ply	polar	pontificate	
pm	pole	pontoon	
pneumatic	polemic	pony	
pneumonia	police	pool	
poach	policeman	poor	
poacher	policy	poorer	
pocket	polish	poorest	
pod	polite	poorly	
poem	politely	pop	
poet	political	Pope	
poetess	politically	poplar	
poetic	politician	poplin	
poetical	politics	populace	
poetically	poll	popular	
poetry	pollute	popularity	
poignant	pollution	population	
point	polytechnic	porcelain	
pointer	polythene	porch	
pointless	pomp	pore	

139

pork	possess	postponement
porous	possession	postscript
porpoise	possessive	postulate
porridge	possessor	postulant
port	possibility	posture
portable	possible	posy
portal	possibly	pot
portend	post	potash
portent	postage	potassium
portentous	postal	potato
portentously	postcard	potent
porter	postdated	potentate
portfolio	poster	potential
portico	posterior	potentially
portion	posterity	pothole
portrait	postgraduate	potion
portraiture	posthumous	potter
portray	posthumously	pottery
pose	postman	pouch
poser	postmark	poultice
poseur	postmaster	poultry
position	post-mortem	pounce
positive	postpaid	pound
positively	postpone	poundage

140

pour	prayer	preclude
pout	preach	precocious
poverty	preacher	preconception
powder	preamble	preconcerted
power	precarious	predatory
powerful	precariously	predecessor
powerfully	precast	predestined
powerless	precaution	predetermined
practicability	precautionary	predicament
practicable	precede	predicate
practical	precedence	predict
practically	precedent	predictably
practice practise	precept	prediction
practitioner	precinct	predominance
pragmatic	precious	predominant
pragmatically	precipice	predominantly
prairie	precipitant	pre-eminent
praise	precipitantly	pre-eminently
praiseworthy	precipitate	pre-empt
prance	precipitous	preface
prank	précis	prefect
prate	precise	prefer
prattle	precisely	preferable
pray	precision	preferably

preference		prepaid		preside	
preferential		preparation		presidency	
preferment		preparatory		president	
prefigure		prepare		presidential	
prefix		prepay		press	
pregnant		preponderance		pressure	
prehistoric		preposition		prestige	
prejudge		preposterous		prestressed	
prejudice		prerequisite		presumably	
prejudicial		prerogative		presume	
prejudicially		Presbyterian		presumption	
prelate		prescient		presumptive	
preliminary		prescribe		presumptuous	
prelude		prescription		presuppose	
premature		presence		pretence pretense	
prematurely		present		pretend	
premeditate		presentable		pretentious	
premeditation		presentably		pretext	
premier		presentation		pretty	
premise		presentiment		prevail	
premises		presently		prevalence	
premium		preservation		prevalent	
premonition		preservative		prevaricate	
preoccupied		preserve		prevent	

142

preventative		primrose		probably	
prevention		primus		probate	
preventive		prince		probation	
preview		princess		probationary	
previous		principal		probe	
previously		principality		probity	
pre-war		principally		problem	
prey		principle		problematic	
price		print		procedural	
priceless		printer		procedure	
prick		prior		proceed	
prickle		priority		process	
pride		prism		procession	
priest		prison		proclaim	
prig		prisoner		proclamation	
prim		privacy		procrastinate	
primarily		private		procreate	
primary		privately		proctor	
primate		privation		procure	
prime		privilege		prod	
primer		prize		prodigal	
primeval		pro		prodigous	
primitive		probability		prodigously	
primogeniture		probable		prodigy	

produce

producer

product

production

productive

productively

productivity

profane

profanity

profess

profession

professional

profes-
sionalism

professor

professorship

proffer

proficiency

proficient

proficiently

profile

profit

profitable

profitably

profligate

pro-forma

profound

profoundly

profuse

profusion

progeny

prognosis

prognosticate

programme
program

progress

progressive

progressively

prohibit

prohibition

prohibitive

prohibitively

project

projection

projector

proletarian

proletariat

proliferate

prolific

prologue

prolong

promenade

prominence

prominent

prominently

promiscuous

promise

promissory

promontory

promote

promoter

promotion

promotional

prompt

promptitude

promptly

promulgate

prone

prong

pronoun

pronounce

pronounce-
ment

pronunciation

proof

144

prop		proposition		protect	
propaganda		propound		protection	
propagate		proprietary		protectionist	
propel		proprietor		protective	
propeller		propriety		protectively	
propensity		propulsion		protector	
proper		prorogue		protectorate	
properly		prosaic		protégé	
property		proscribe		protein	
prophecy		prose		protest	
prophesy		prosecute		Protestant	
prophet		prosecution		protestation	
prophetic		prosecutor		protocol	
prophetically		prospect		protracted	
propitiate		prospective		protrude	
propitious		prospectively		protuberant	
propitiously		prospectus		proud	
proponent		prosper		proudly	
proportion		prosperity		provable	
proportional		prosperous		prove	
proportionate		prosperously		proven	
propor-tionately		prostrate		proverb	
proposal		prostration		proverbial	
propose		protagonist		proverbially	

145

provide		pseudo		pulley	
providence		pseudonym		pullover	
provident		psychiatric		pulmonary	
province		psychic		pulp	
provincial		psychological		pulpit	
provision		psychologist		pulse	
provisional		psychology		pumice	
provisionally		psychotherapy		pump	
provocation		ptomaine		pun	
provocative		puberty		punch	
provocatively		public		punctilious	
provoke		publication		punctual	
provost		publicist		punctuality	
prow		publicity		punctually	
prowess		publicize		punctuate	
prowl		publicly		punctuation	
proximity		publish		puncture	
proxy		publisher		pundit	
prudence		pudding		pungent	
prudent		puddle		punish	
prudently		puerile		punishment	
prune		puff		punitive	
pry		pugnacious		punt	
psalm		pull		puny	

146

pup		purity		pursuit		
pupil		purloin		pus		
puppet		purple		push		
puppy		purport		*put*		
purchase		purpose		putative		
purchaser		purposely		putrid		
pure		purr		putt		
purely		purse		putty		
purgatory		purser		puzzle		
purge		pursuance		pyjámas		
purification		pursuant		pylon		
purify		pursue		pyramid		
Puritan		pursuer		pyre		

Q

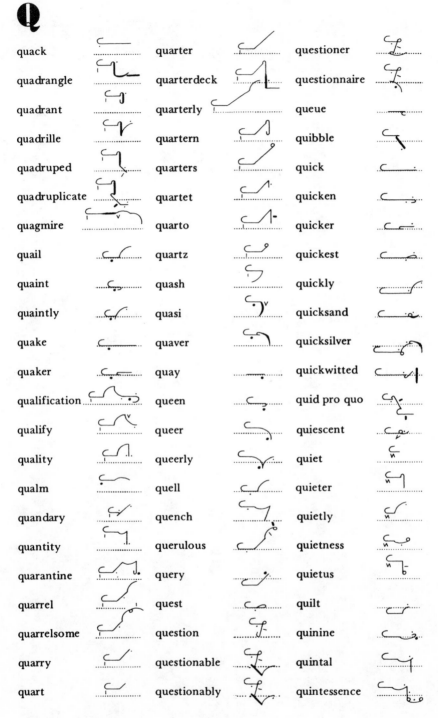

quack	quarter	questioner
quadrangle	quarterdeck	questionnaire
quadrant	quarterly	queue
quadrille	quartern	quibble
quadruped	quarters	quick
quadruplicate	quartet	quicken
quagmire	quarto	quicker
quail	quartz	quickest
quaint	quash	quickly
quaintly	quasi	quicksand
quake	quaver	quicksilver
quaker	quay	quickwitted
qualification	queen	quid pro quo
qualify	queer	quiescent
quality	queerly	quiet
qualm	quell	quieter
quandary	quench	quietly
quantity	querulous	quietness
quarantine	query	quietus
quarrel	quest	quilt
quarrelsome	question	quinine
quarry	questionable	quintal
quart	questionably	quintessence

quintet		quitter		quorum		
quip		quiver		quota		
quire		quixotic		quotation		
quit		quiz		quote		
quite		quizzical		quoter		
quittance		quoit		quotient		

R

rabbi	radioactive	rainy
rabbit	radiogram	raise
rabble	radiologist	raisin
rabid	radiotherapy	rake
rabies	radish	rally
race	radium	ram
racehorse	radius	ramble
racer	raffle	rambler
racial	raft	ramification
racially	rafter	ramp
rack	rag	rampage
racket	rage	rampant
racy	ragged	rampart
radar	raid	ramshackle
radiance	rail	ran
radiant	railroad	ranch
radiantly	railway	rancid
radiate	raiment	rancour rancor
radiation	rain	rand
radiator	rainbow	random
radical	raincoat	rang
radically	rainfall	range
radio	rainproof	ranger

rank	rat(e)able	reach
rankle	ratepayer	react
ransack	rather	reaction
ransom	ratification	reactionary
rant	ratify	reactivate
rap	rating	read
rapacious	ratio	readable
rapacity	ration	reader
rape	rational	readier
rapid	rationalization	readily
rapidity	rationally	readiness
rapidly	rattle	readjust
rapport	raucous	readjustment
rapt	ravage	readmission
rapture	rave	readmit
rare	ravenous	ready
rarity	ravine	reaffirm
rascal	ravish	real
rash	raw	realism
rashly	ray	realist
raspberry	rayon	realistic
rat	raze	realistically
ratchet	razor	reality
rate	re	realization

realize		rebellion		recess	
really		rebellious		recession	
realm		rebound		recharge	
realty		rebuff		recipe	
ream		rebuild		recipient	
reap		rebuilt		reciprocal	
reappear		rebuke		reciprocate	
reappearance		rebut		reciprocity	
reappoint		recalcitrant		recital	
reappointment		recall		recitation	
reapportion		recant		recite	
rear		recapitulate		reckless	
rearrange		recapitulation		reckon	
rearrangement		recapture		reclaim	
reason		recast		reclamation	
reasonable		recede		recline	
reasonably		receipt		recluse	
reassemble		receive		recognition	
reassert		receiver		recognizance	
reassurance		recent		recognize	
reassure		recently		recoil	
rebate		receptacle		recollect	
rebel, *n & adj*		reception		recollection	
rebel, *v*		receptive		recommence	

recommend	recruit	redress
recommen-dation	rectangular	reduce
recompense	rectify	reduction
reconcile	rectitude	redundant
reconciliation	rector	reed
recondite	rectum	reef
reconnaissance	recumbent	reek
reconnoitre reconnoiter	recuperate	reel
reconquer	recuperation	re-elect
reconsider	recur	re-election
reconsideration	recurrence	re-enact
reconstitute	recurrent	re-entrant
reconstruct	red	re-establish
reconstruction	redeem	re-examine
record	redemption	refectory
recorder	red-handed	refer
recount	red-hot	referee
recoup	redistribute	reference
recourse	redolent	referendum
recover	redouble	refine
recoverable	redoubt	refinement
recovery	redoubtable	refiner
recrimination	redound	refinery
recrudescence	redraft	reflation

reflect		refute		regrettably	
reflection		regain		regular	
reflective		regal		regularity	
reflectively		regale		regularly	
reflex		regard		regulate	
reform		regardless		regulation	
reformation		regency		regulator	
reformatory		regenerate		regulatory	
reformer		regent		regurgitate	
refraction		regime		rehabilitate	
refractory		regimen		rehabilitation	
refrain		regiment		rehash	
refresh		regimental		rehearsal	
refreshment		region		rehearse	
refrigerate		regional		rehouse	
refrigeration		regionally		reign	
refrigerator		register		reimburse	
refuge		registrar		reimburse-ment	
refugee		registration		rein	
refund		registry		reindeer	
refurbish		regret		reinforce	
refusal		regretful		reinstate	
refuse		regretfully		reinstatement	
refutation		regrettable		reiterate	

reiteration		reliably		remind	
reject		reliance		reminder	
rejection		reliant		reminisce	
rejoice		relic		reminiscence	
rejoinder		relief		reminiscent	
rejuvenate		relieve		remiss	
relapse		religion		remission	
relate		religious		remit	
relation		relinquish		remittance	
relationship		relish		remnant	
relative		reluctance		remonstrance	
relatively		reluctant		remonstrate	
relax		reluctantly		remorse	
relaxation		rely		remorseless	
relay		remain		remote	
release		remainder		remotely	
relegate		remand		removable	
relent		remark		removal	
relentless		remarkable		remove	
relentlessly		remarkably		remover	
relevancy		remedial		remunerate	
relevant		remedy		remuneration	
reliability		remember		remunerative	
reliable		remembrance		remuneratively	

155

renaissance	repeatedly	representative
rend	repel	reprieve
render	repellant	reprimand
rendezvous	repent	reprisal
renegade	repentance	reproach
renewal	repentant	reproachful
renounce	repercussion	reproachfully
renovate	repertoire	reprobate
renovation	repertory	reproduce
renown	repetition	reproduction
rent	repine	reprove
rental	replenish	reptile
renunciation	replete	republic
reorientate	repletion	republican
reorganiza- tion	replica	repudiate
repair	reply	repudiation
reparable	report	repugnance
reparation	reporter	repugnant
repartee	repose	repulse
repast	repository	repulsion
repatriate	reprehend	repulsive
repayment	reprehen- sible	reputable
repeal	represent	reputation
repeat	representation	repute

request		residual		respectable	
requiem		residuary		respectably	
require		residue		respectful	
requirement		resign		respectfully	
requisite		resignation		respective	
requisition		resignedly		respectively	
requite		resilience		respiration	
rescind		resilient		respirator	
rescue		resin		respiratory	
rescuer		resist		respire	
research		resistance		resplendent	
resemblance		resistant		resplendently	
resemble		resolute		respond	
resent		resolutely		response	
resentful		resolution		responsibility	
resentment		resolve		responsible	
reservation		resonant		responsibly	
reserve		resort		responsive	
reservoir		resoundingly		restart	
reside		resource		restaurant	
residence		resourceful		restaurateur	
residency		resourcefully		restful	
resident		respect		restfully	
residential		respectability		restitution	

157

restive		retaliatory		return			
restless		retard		returnable			
restoration		retch		reunion			
restorative		retention		reunite			
restore		retentive		revaluation			
restrain		reticence		reveal			
restraint		reticent		revel			
restrict		retina		revelation			
restriction		retinue		revelry			
restrictive		retire		revenge			
result		retirement		revenue			
resultant		retort		reverberate			
resume		retouch		reverberation			
resumé		retrace		revere			
resumption		retract		reverence			
resurgence		retreat		reverend			
resurrection		retrench		reverent			
resuscitate		retrenchment		reversal			
resuscitation		retribution		reverse			
retail		retrieve		reversible			
retailer		retroactive		reversion			
retain		retrograde		revert			
retaliate		retrogressive		revetment			
retaliation		retrospect		review			

158

reviewer		rheumatism		right		
revile		rhyme rime		righteous		
revise		rhythm		righteousness		
revision		rib		rightful		
revival		ribald		rightfully		
revive		ribbon		right-hand		
revocation		rice		rightly		
revoke		rich		rigid		
revolt		richer		rigidity		
revolution		richest		rigorous		
revolutionary		rid		rigorously		
revolutionize		riddance		rigour rigor		
revolve		riddle		rile		
revolver		ride		rim		
revue		rider		rind		
revulsion		ridge		ring		
reward		ridicule		ringer		
reword		ridiculous		ringlet		
re-write		riding		rink		
re-written		rife		rinse		
rhapsody		riffraff		riot		
rhetoric		rifle		rioter		
rhetorical		rift		riotous		
rheumatic		rig		rip		

ripe	robber	romper
ripen	robbery	roof
riper	robe	roofless
ripest	robin	rook
riposte	robot	room
ripple	robust	roomy
rise	rock	roost
risen	rocker	rooster
risk	rockery	root
risky	rocket	rope
rite	rod	rosary
ritual	rode	rose
rival	rodent	roster
rivalry	roe	rostrum
river	rogue	rosy
rivet	roguish	rot
road	role	rota
roadster	roll	rotary
roadway	roller	rotate
roam	roman	rotation
roan	romance	rotatory
roar	romantic	rote
roast	romantically	rotor
rob	romp	rotten

160

rotund	rubber	rule
rotundity	rubbish	ruler
rouble	rubble	rum
rouge	rubicund	rumble
rough	rubric	ruminate
roughen	ruby	rummage
rougher	ruction	rumour / rumor
roughest	rudder	rump
roughly	rude	rumple
round	rudeness	run
roundabout	rudiment	rung
rouse	rudimentary	runner
rout	rue	runway
route	rueful	rupture
routine	ruefully	rural
rove	ruff	ruse
rover	ruffian	rush
row (a tier)	ruffle	rusk
row (a noise)	rug	russet
rowdy	rugged	rust
royal	ruin	rustic
royally	ruination	rusticate
royalty	ruinous	rustle
rub	ruinously	rustless

| rustproof | ⟨shorthand⟩ | rut | ⟨shorthand⟩ | ruthlessly | ⟨shorthand⟩ |
| rusty | ⟨shorthand⟩ | ruthless | ⟨shorthand⟩ | rye | ⟨shorthand⟩ |

S

Sabbath		sahib	salute
sabbatical		said	salvage
sabotage		sail	salvation
saccharin(e)		sailor	salve
sack		saint	same
sacrament		saintly	sample
sacred		sake	sanatorium
sacrifice		salad	sanctify
sad		salary	sanctimonious
sadden		sale	sanction
saddle		saleable salable	sanctuary
sadist		salesman	sand
sadly		saleswoman	sandal
safe		salient	sandwich
safeguard		saline	sandy
safely		saliva	sane
safer		sallow	sanely
safest		salmon	sang
safety		saloon	sanguinary
sag		salt	sanguine
sagacious		salubrious	sanitarium
sagacity		salutary	sanitary
sage		salutation	sanitation

sanity		Saturday		scalpel		
sank		sauce		scamp		
sap		saucepan		scamper		
sapphire		saucer		scan		
sarcasm		saunter		scandal		
sarcastic		sausage		scandalous		
sarcastically		savage		scandalously		
sardine		savagely		scant		
sardonic		savagery		scantily		
sash		save		scanty		
sat		saviour		scapegoat		
satanic		savour savor		scar		
satchel		savoury		scarce		
satellite		saw		scarcity		
satiate		sawdust		scare		
satin		sawn		scarf		
satire		saxophone		scarlet		
satirical		say		scathing		
satisfaction		scab		scathingly		
satisfactorily		scaffold		scatter		
satisfactory		scald		scavenger		
satisfy		scale		scene		
saturate		scallop		scenery		
saturation		scalp		scenic		

164

scenically	scintillating	scratch	
scent	scissors	scrawl	
sceptic skeptic	scoff	scream	
sceptical skeptical	scold	screech	
scepticism skepticism	scoop	screed	
sceptre scepter	scope	screen	
schedule	scorch	screw	
schedule	score	screwdriver	
scheme	scorn	scribble	
schemer	scornful	scribe	
schism	scorpion	scrimmage	
schizophrenia	scotch	scrimp	
scholar	scotfree	script	
scholarly	scoundrel	scripture	
scholarship	scour	scroll	
scholastic	scourge	scrounge	
school	scout	scrub	
schoolhouse	scowl	scrum	
schooner	scraggy	scruple	
sciatica	scramble	scrupulous	
science	scrap	scrutinize	
scientific	scrape	scrutiny	
scientifically	scrapheap	scuffle	
scientist	scrappy	sculptor	

165

sculpture		seaworthy		secular	
scum		secede		secure	
scurrilous		secession		securely	
scurry		seclude		security	
scurvy		seclusion		sedan	
scuttle		second		sedate	
scythe		secondary		sedately	
sea		second-hand		sedentary	
seafaring		secondly		sediment	
seal		second-rate		sedition	
sea-level		secrecy		seditious	
sealing-wax		secret		see	
seam		secretarial		seed	
seaman		secretariat		seedling	
seance		secretary		seek	
sear		secrete		seem	
search		secretion		seemingly	
searcher		secretive		seemly	
searchingly		secretively		seen	
seashore		sect		seep	
season		sectarian		seer	
seasonable		section		seethe	
seasonal		sectional		segment	
seaweed		sector		segregate	

166

segregation		sell		sensitive	
seismic		seller		sensitively	
seize		selves		sensual	
seizure		semantics		sent	
seldom		semblance		sentence	
select		semester		sentiment	
selection		semicircle		sentimental	
selective		semicolon		sentinel	
selectively		seminar		sentry	
self		seminary		separate, *adj*	
self-centred		senate		separate, *v*	
self-confident		senator		separation	
self-conscious		send		separator	
self-contained		sender		September	
self-control		senile		sepulchre sepulcher	
self-defence		senior		sequel	
self-discipline		seniority		sequence	
self-explanatory		sensation		sequester	
self-help		sensational		sequestrate	
selfish		sense		serenade	
selfishly		senseless		serene	
selfishness		senselessly		serenely	
self-respect		sensibility		serenity	
self-willed		sensible		serge	

167

sergeant		seventeenth	17(or	shadowy
serial		seventh	7(or	shaft
series		seventieth	70(or	shaggy
serious		seventy	70 or	shah
seriously		sever		shake
seriousness		*several*		shaken
sermon		*severally*		shaker
serpent		severance		shakier
serrated		severe		*shall*
servant		severely		shallow
serve		severity		sham
service		sew		shame
serviceable		sewer		shameful
serviceman		sewer		shamefully
servile		sewerage		shameless
servility		sewn		shamelessly
servitude		sex		shampoo
session		sexton		shank
set		shabbily		shape
settle		shabby		shapeless
settlement		shack		shapely
settler		shackle		share
seven		shade		shareholder
seventeen		shadow		shark

168

sharp		shell		shirk	
sharpen		shellfish		shirt	
sharper		shelter		shiver	
sharpest		shelve		shoal	
sharply		shepherd		shock	
sharp-witted		sherbet		shod	
shatter		sheriff		shoddily	
shave		sherry		shoe	
shawl		shield		shoemaker	
she		shift		shoe-string	
sheaf		shiftless		shone	
shear		shifty		shook	
sheath		shilling		shoot	
sheathe		shimmer		shooter	
sheaves		shin		shop	
shed		shine		shore	
sheen		shingle		shorn	
sheep		shiny		short	
sheepish		ship		shortage	
sheepishly		shipbuilding		shortcoming	
sheer		shipment		shorten	
sheet		shipowner		shorter	
shekels		shipper		shortest	
shelf		shire		shorthand	

169

shortly		shrinkage		siege	
shortsighted		shrivel		sieve	
shortsightedly		shroud		sift	
short-term		shrub		sigh	
shot		shrug		sight	
should		shrunk		sight-seeing	
shoulder		shudder		sign	
shout		shuffle		signal	
shove		shun		signatory	
shovel		shunt		signature	
show		shut		signer	
shower		shutter		significance	
showmanship		shuttle		significant	
shown		shy		significantly	
showroom		shyly		signify	
shrank		sick		silence	
shred		sicken		silent	
shrew		sickle		silently	
shrewd		sickly		silhouette	
shriek		sickness		silicon	
shrill		side		silk	
shrimp		sidewalk		silkworm	
shrine		sideways		silly	
shrink		sidle		silo	

170

silt		sinew		sit		
silver		sinewy		site		
similar		sinful		situate		
similarity		sing		situation		
similarly		singe		six	6. or	
simile		singer		sixteen	16. or	
similitude		single		sixteenth	16(or	
simmer		singular		sixth	6(or	
simper		singularity		sixty	60. or	
simple		singularly		size		
simpler		sinister		sizeable		
simplest		sink		sizzle		
simpleton		sinner		skate		
simplicity		sinus		skater		
simplify		sip		skein		
simply		siphon		skeleton		
simulate		sir		sketch		
simultaneous		sire		ski		
sin		siren		skid		
since		sirloin		skiff		
sincere		sisal		skilful		
				skillful		
sincerely		sister		skilfully		
sincerity		sister-*in*-law		skill		
sinecure		sisterly		skim		

171

skimp		slang		slept		
skin		slant		slew		
skinflint		slap		slice		
skinny		slash		slick		
skip		slate		slid		
skipper		slaughter		slide		
skirmish		slaughterhouse		slight		
skirt		slave		slightly		
skit		slavery		slim		
skittle		slavish		slime		
skulduggery		slavishly		sling		
skulk		slay		slink		
skull		slayer		slip		
skunk		sledge		slipper		
sky		sleek		slippery		
skyscraper		sleep		slipshod		
slab		sleeper		slit		
slack		sleeplessness		slither		
slacken		sleepwalking		sliver		
slag		sleepy		slobber		
slain		sleet		slog		
slam		sleeve		slogan		
slander		sleigh		slop		
slanderous		slender		slope		

slot	small	smoulder / smolder
sloth	smaller	smudge
slothful	smallest	smug
slouch	smart	smuggle
slough (a bog)	smarten	smuggler
slovenly	smarter	smugly
slow	smartest	smut
slowly	smartly	snack
sludge	smash	snag
slug	smattering	snail
sluggard	smear	snake
sluggish	smell	snap
sluggishly	smile	snare
sluice	smilingly	snarl
slum	smirk	snatch
slumber	smith	sneak
slump	smock	sneer
slung	smoke	sneeringly
slur	smoker	sneeze
slush	smooth	sniff
slut	smoother	snigger
sly	smoothest	snip
slyly	smoothly	snivel
smack	smother	snob

173

snobbish		soccer		sole	
snobbishly		sociable		solecism	
snooker		social		solely	
snoop		socialism		solemn	
snore		socialist		solemnity	
snort		society		solemnization	
snout		sociology		solemnly	
snow		sock		solicit	
snowfall		socket		solicitor	
snowplough		sod		solicitude	
snowshoes		soda		solid	
snowstorm		sodden		solidarity	
snub		sodium		solidify	
snuff		sofa		solidity	
snug		soft		solidly	
so		soften		soliloquy	
soak		softly		solitary	
soap		soggy		solitude	
soar		soil		solo	
sob		solace		soloist	
sober		solar		solstice	
soberly		sold		solubility	
sobriety		solder	or	soluble	
so-called		soldier		solution	

174

solve		sooty		sourly		
solvency		sop		south		
solvent		sophisticated		southeast		
sombre somber		sophistication		southeastern		
some		sophistry		southern		
somebody		sophomore		southerner		
somehow		soporific		southward		
someone		soprano		southwest		
somersault		sorcerer		southwestern		
something		sordid		souvenir		
sometime		sore		sovereign		
somewhat		sorely		sovereignty		
somewhere		sorrow		sow (a pig)		
somnolent		sorrowful		sow (to scatter)		
son		sorry		sower		
song		sort		sown		
son-in-law		sought		soya-bean		
sonnet		soul		space		
sonorous		sound		space-craft		
soon		sounder		spacious		
sooner		soundest		spade		
soonest		soup		span		
soot		sour		spangle		
soothe		source		spaniel		

175

spank		specialist		speed	
spanner		speciality		speedily	
spar		specialize		speedometer	
spare		specially		speedy	
sparingly	*or*	specialty		spell	
spark		specie		spend	
sparkle		specific		spent	
sparrow		specifically		sphere	
sparse		specification		spherical	
sparsely		specify		sphinx	
sparsity		specimen		spice	
Spartan		speck		spicy	
spasm		speckle		spider	
spasmodic		spectacle		spike	
spasmodically		spectacular		spill	
spastic		spectator		spilt	
spat		spectre specter		spin	
spatter		spectrum		spinach	
spawn		speculate		spinal	
speak		speculation		spindle	
speaker		speculative		spindrier	
spear		speculator		spine	
spearhead		sped		spineless	
special		speech		spinster	

176

spiral	spokesman	sprint
spire	sponge	sprite
spirit	sponsor	sprout
spiritedly	spontaneous	spruce
spiritual	spontaneously	sprung
spit	spool	spry
spite	sporadic	spun
spiteful	sporadically	spur
spitefulness	sport	spurious
splash	sportsman	spuriously
splay	spot	spurn
spleen	spotless	spurt
splendid	spouse	spy
splendidly	spout	squabble
splendour splendor	sprain	squad
splice	sprang	squadron
splint	sprawl	squalid
splinter	spray	squall
split	spread	squalor
splutter	spree	squander
spoil	sprig	square
spoilt	sprightly	squash
spoke	spring	squat
spoken	sprinkle	squaw

squawk	staid	star
squeak	stain	starboard
squeal	stainless	starch
squeamish	stair	stare
squeamishly	stake	stark
squeeze	stalactite	starkly
squib	stalagmite	starling
squint	stale	starry-*eyed*
squire	stalk	star-spangled
squirm	stall	start
squirrel	stalwart	starter
squirt	stamina	startle
stab	stammer	starvation
stability	stamp	starve
stabilize	stampede	state
stable	stance	statement
stack	stand	statesman
stadium	standard	static
staff	standardization	station
stag	standardize	stationary
stage	standpoint	stationer
stagger	standstill	stationery
stagnant	stank	statistical
stagnation	staple	statistically

statistician		steel		steward	
statistic		steep		stewardess	
statue		steeple		stewardship	
statuesque		steeply		stick	
stature		steer		stickily	
status		steerage		stiff	
statute		stem		stiffen	
statutory		stench		stifle	
staunch		stencil		stigmatize	
stave		stenographer		stile	
stay		stenography		still	
stead		step		stimulant	
steadfast stedfast		stereo		stimulate	
steadfastly		stereotyped		stimulation	
steadily		sterile		stimulus	
steady		sterility		sting	
steak		sterilize		stingily	
steal		sterling		stingy	
stealth		stern		stink	
stealthily		sternly		stint	
stealthy		stet		stipend	
steam		stetson		stipulate	
steamer		stevedore		stipulation	
steed		stew		stir	

179

stirrup		stork		strap	
stitch		storm		strategically	
stock		story		strategy	
stockbroker		stout		stratification	
stockholder		stoutly		stratosphere	
stockist		stove		stratum	
stocktaking		stow		straw	
stoker		stowage		strawberry	
stole		straddle		stray	
stolen		straggle		streak	
stolid		straight		stream	
stomach		straighten		streamline	
stone		straight- forward		street	
stonily		strain		strength	
stood		strainer		strengthen	
stooge		strait		strenuous	
stool		straitlaced		strenuously	
stoop		strand		stress	
stop		strange		stretch	
stoppage		strangely		stretcher	
stopper		stranger		strew	
stopwatch		strangest		stricken	
storage		strangle		strict	
store		stranglehold		stricter	

180

strictest	strongly	stump	
strictly	strove	stun	
stricture	struck	stung	
stride	structural	stunt	
strident	structure	stupefaction	
stridently	struggle	stupefy	
strife	strum	stupendous	
strike	strung	stupendously	
striker	strut	stupid	
string	stub	stupidity	
stringency	stubble	stupor	
stringent	stubborn	sturdy	
stringently	stubbornly	stutter	
strip	stubbornness	sty	
stripe	stuck	style	
stripling	stud	stylish	
strive	student	styptic	
strode	studio	suave	
stroke	studious	subcommittee	
stroll	studiously	subconscious	
strong	study	subdue	
stronger	stuff	subject	
strongest	stultify	subjection	
stronghold	stumble	subjective	

subjectively		substantive		succumb	
subjunctive		substitute		such	
sublime		substitution		suck	
submission		subterfuge		suckle	
submit		subterranean		suction	
subordinate		subtle		sudden	
subpoena subpena		subtlety		suddenly	
subscribe		subtract		sue	
subscriber		subtraction		suède	
subscription		suburb		suet	
subsequent		suburban		suffer	
subsequently		subversion		sufferance	
subservient		subvert		suffice	
subserviently		subway		sufficiency	
subside		succeed		sufficient	
subsidence		success		sufficiently	
subsidiary		successful		suffix	
subsidize		successfully		suffocate	
subsidy		succession		suffocation	
subsist		successive		suffrage	
subsistence		successor		suffragette	
substance		succinct		sugar	
substantial		succinctly		suggest	
substantiate		succour succor		suggestion	

182

suggestive	summon	superiority
suicide	sump	superlative
suit	sumptuous	supernatural
suitability	sumptuously	supernumerary
suitable	sun	supersede
suite	Sunday	superstition
suitor	sunder	superstitious
sulky	sundry	supervise
sullen	sung	supervision
sulphate	sunk	supervisor
sulphide	sunken	supervisory
sulphona-mide	sunny	supper
sulphur	sup	supplant
sulphuric	super	supple
sulphurous	superannuation	supplement
sultan	superb	supplemental
sultry	superbly	supplemen-tary
sum	supercilious	suppliant
summarily	superficial	supplicant
summarize	superfluous	supplicate
summary	superhuman	supplication
summer	superintend	supplier
summer-house	superintendent	supply
summit	superior	support

183

supportable		surmount		sustenance		
supporter		surname		swagger		
suppose		surpass		swallow		
supposition		surplice		swam		
suppress		surplus		swamp		
suppression		surprise		swan		
supremacy		surrender		swap		
supreme		surreptitious		swarm		
supremely		surreptitiously		swarthy		
surcharge		surround		swathe		
sure		survey		sway		
surely		surveyor		swear		
surer		survival		sweat		
surest		survive		sweater		
surety		survivor		sweep		
surf		susceptible		sweeper		
surface		suspect		sweet		
surfeit		suspend		sweeten		
surge		suspense		sweeter		
surgeon		suspension		sweetest		
surgery		suspicion		sweetly		
surgical		suspicious		sweetness		
surly		suspiciously		swell		
surmise		sustain		swelter		

184

swept		swoop		symposium		
swerve		sword		symptom		
swift		swore		synagogue		
swifter		sworn		synchronize		
swiftest		swum		syncopation		
swiftly		swung		syndicate		
swill		syllable		synonym		
swim		syllabus		synonymous		
swimmer		symbol		synopsis		
swindle		symbolic		syntax		
swine		symbolically		synthesis		
swing		symbolize		synthetic		
swipe		symmetrical		syringe		
swirl		symmetry		syrup		
switch		sympathetic		system		
swivel		sympathize		systematic		
swollen		sympathy		systematical		
swoon		symphony		systematically		

T

tab		tactless		tame
table		tactlessly		tamper
tableau		tag		tan
tablecloth		tail		tandem
tablespoon		tail-end		tang
tablet		tail-light		tangent
tabloid		tailor		tangible
taboo		tailor-made		tangibly
tabular		tail-piece		tangle
tabulate		taint		tank
tabulation		take		tankard
tabulator		taken		tanker
tacit		take-off		tanner
tacitly		take-over		tantalize
taciturn		talcum		tantamount
tack		tale		tantrum
tackle		talent		tap
tact		talk		tape
tactful		talkative		taper
tactfully		talker		tape-recorder
tactically		tall		tapestry
tactician		tallow		tar
tactics		tally		tardily

tardiness	taught	tearful
tardy	taunt	tearfully
tare	taut	tease
target	tautology	teaspoon
tariff	tavern	technical
tarmac	tawdry	technicality
tarnish	tax	technically
tarpaulin	taxable	technician
tarry	taxation	technique
tart	tax-collector	technology
tartan	taxes	tedious
tartar	tax-free	tediously
tartaric	taxi	tedium
task	taxidermy	teem
taskmaster	taxpayer	teenager
tassel	teach	teeth
taste	teacher	teethe
tasteful	teach-*in*	teetotal
tastefully	team	teetotal(l)er
tasteless	teamster	tele-
		communication
tasty	team-work	telegram
tatter	teapot	telegraph
tattle	tear, *n*	telegraphic
tattoo	tear, *v*	telegraphist

187

telegraphy		temporarily		tent	
telepathy		temporary		tentacle	
telephone		tempt		tentative	
telephonist		temptation		tentatively	
teleprinter		ten		tenterhooks	
telescope		tenable		tenth	
teletype		tenacious		tenure	
television		tenaciously		tepid	
telex		tenacity		tepidly	
tell		tenancy		term	
teller		tenant		terminal	
tell-tale		tend		terminate	
temerity		tendency		termination	
temper		tender		terminology	
temperament		tenderly		terminus	
tempera-mental		tendon		terrace	
tempera-mentally		tendril		terrain	
temperance		tenement		terrestrial	
temperate		tenet		terrible	
temperature		tenfold		terribly	
tempest		tennis		terrier	
tempestuous		tenor		terrific	
temple		tense		terrifically	
temporal		tension		terrify	

territorial		texture	
territory		than	
terror		thank	
terrorist		thankful	
terse		thankfully	
tersely		thankfulness	
tertiary		thankless	
test		thanks	
testament		thanksgiving	
testator		that	
testatrix		thatch	
tester		thatcher	
testify		thaw	
testily		the	
testimonial		theatre theater	
testimony		theatrical	
testy		thee	
tetanus		theft	
tetchy		their	
tether		theirs	
text		them	
textbook		theme	
textile		themselves	
textual		then	

thence	
thenceforth	
thence-forward	
theodolite	
theological	
theology	
theorem	
theoretical	
theoretically	
theorist	
theory	
there	
thereabouts	
thereafter	
thereat	
thereby	
therefore	
therein	
thereof	
thereon	
thereto	
thereupon	
therewith	
therm	

thermo-dynamics		third	thoughtlessly
thermometer		third-rate	thoughtlessness
thermostat		thirst	thousand
these		thirsty	thousandfold
thesis		thirteen or 13	thousandth
they		thirtieth or 30	thrash
thick		thirty or 30	thread
thicken		this	threadbare
thicker		thistle	threat
thickest		thong	threaten
thicket		thorn	three
thickly		thorny	three-quarters
thief		thorough	thresh
thieves		thoroughbred	threshold
thigh		thoroughfare	threw
thimble		thoroughly	thrice
thin		those	thrift
thine		thou	thrifty
thing		though	thrill
think		thought	thrive
thinker		thoughtful	throat
thinly		thoughtfully	throb
thinner		thoughtfulness	throes
thinnest		thoughtless	throne

190

throng		tidily		time-saving	
throttle		tidings		time-server	
through		tidy		time-signal	
throughout		tie		time-switch	
throw		tier (a row)		timetable	
thrown		tiff		timid	
thrush		tiger		timidity	
thrust		tight		timidly	
thud		tighten		timorous	
thug		tightly		tin	
thumb		tightness		tincture	
thump		tigress		tinder	
thunder		tile		tinge	
thunderbolt		till		tingle	
thunderstorm		tillage		tinker	
Thursday		tilt		tinkle	
thus		timber		tinsel	
thwart		time		tint	
tick		time-bomb		tiny	
ticket		time-consuming		tip	
tickle		time-honoured		tippler	
ticklish		timekeeper		tipsy	
tidal		timeless		tirade	
tide		timely		tire	

tireless	tolerable	top	
tiresome	tolerably	topaz	
tiro / tyro	tolerance	topic	
tissue	tolerate	topical	
titanic	toleration	topically	
tithe	toll	topography	
titivate	tomato	topple	
title	tomb	torch	
titter	tombstone	tore	
tittle-tattle	tomorrow	torment	
titular	ton	torn	
to	tone	tornado	
toad	tongs	torpedo	
toast	tongue	torpid	
tobacco	tonic	torrent	
toboggan	tonight	torrential	
today	tonnage	torrid	
toe	tonsil	torso	
toffee	too	tort	
together	took	tortoise	
toil	tool	tortuous	
toilet	toot	torture	
token	tooth	toss	
told	toothache	tot	

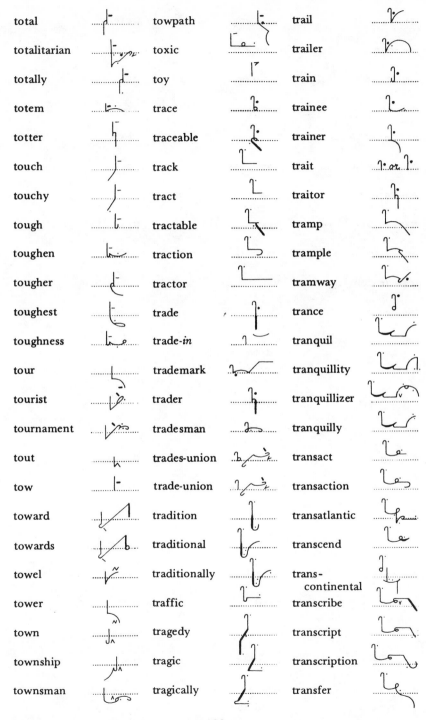

total		towpath		trail	
totalitarian		toxic		trailer	
totally		toy		train	
totem		trace		trainee	
totter		traceable		trainer	
touch		track		trait	
touchy		tract		traitor	
tough		tractable		tramp	
toughen		traction		trample	
tougher		tractor		tramway	
toughest		trade		trance	
toughness		trade-*in*		tranquil	
tour		trademark		tranquillity	
tourist		trader		tranquillizer	
tournament		tradesman		tranquilly	
tout		trades-union		transact	
tow		trade-union		transaction	
toward		tradition		transatlantic	
towards		traditional		transcend	
towel		traditionally		trans-continental	
tower		traffic		transcribe	
town		tragedy		transcript	
township		tragic		transcription	
townsman		tragically		transfer	

193

transferee		transpire		treasury		
transferor		transplant		treat		
transfigure		transport		treatise		
transfix		transportation		treatment		
transform		transpose		treaty		
transformation		transverse		treble		
transformer		trap		tree		
transfusion		trash		trek		
transgress		traumatic		tremble		
transgression		travail		tremendous		
transient		travel		tremendously		
transistor		traveller traveler		tremor		
transit		traverse		tremulous		
transition		travesty		trench		
transitional		trawler		trenchant		
transitory		tray		trenchantly		
translate		treacherous		trend		
translation		treacherously		trendy		
translator		treachery		trepidation		
transmission		treacle		trespass		
transmit		tread		tress		
transmitter		treason		trestle		
transparent		treasure		trial		
transparently		treasurer		triangle		

194

triangular		triple		trounce	
tribal		triplets		troupe	
tribe		triplicate		trousers	
tribulation		tripod		trousseau	
tribunal		tripos		trout	
tribune		trite		trowel	
tributary		triumph		truant	
tribute		triumphant		truce	
trick		triumphantly		truck	
trickery		trivial		truckle	
trickle		triviality		truculence	
trickster		trivially		truculent	
tricky		trod		truculently	
trident		trodden		trudge	
trifle		trolley		true	
trigger		trombone		truffle	
trigonometry		troop		truism	
trill		trooper		truly	
trilogy		trophy		trump	
trim		tropical		trumpet	
trinket		trot		truncate	
trio		trouble		truncheon	
trip		troublesome		trundle	
tripe		trough		trunk	

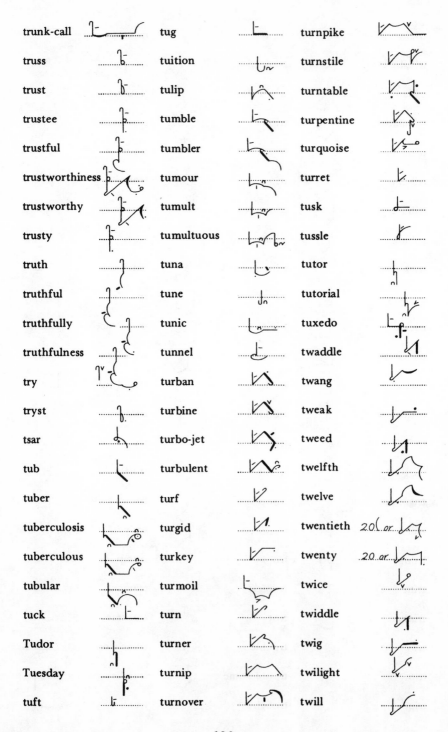

trunk-call	tug	turnpike	
truss	tuition	turnstile	
trust	tulip	turntable	
trustee	tumble	turpentine	
trustful	tumbler	turquoise	
trustworthiness	tumour	turret	
trustworthy	tumult	tusk	
trusty	tumultuous	tussle	
truth	tuna	tutor	
truthful	tune	tutorial	
truthfully	tunic	tuxedo	
truthfulness	tunnel	twaddle	
try	turban	twang	
tryst	turbine	tweak	
tsar	turbo-jet	tweed	
tub	turbulent	twelfth	
tuber	turf	twelve	
tuberculosis	turgid	twentieth	20(or
tuberculous	turkey	twenty	20 or
tubular	turmoil	twice	
tuck	turn	twiddle	
Tudor	turner	twig	
Tuesday	turnip	twilight	
tuft	turnover	twill	

twin		two-seater		typical
twine		two-some		typically
twinge		tycoon		typify
twinkle		type		typist
twirl		typecast		typographer
twist		typewriter		typographical
twit		typewriting		typography
twitch		typewritten		tyrannical
two		typhoid		tyranny
two-faced		typhoon		tyrant
twofold		typhus		tyre

U

ubiquitous	unaccountable	unbalanced
udder	unaccustomed	unbearable
uglier	unacquainted	unbecoming
ugliest	unadaptable	unbeknown
ugly	unaffected	unbelievable
ukelele	unalterable	unbending
ulcer	unanimity	unbiased
ulterior	unanimous	unbleached
ultimate	unanimously	unblemished
ultimately	unanswerable	unbolt
ultimatum	unapproachable	unborn
ultra	unarmed	unbounded
ultramarine	unashamedly	unbreakable
ultra-violet	unasked	unbridled
umbilical	unassisted	unbroken
umbrage	unassuming	unburden
umbrella	unattached	unceasing
umpire	unattainable	uncertain
unabated	unattractive	unchallengeable
unable	unauthorized	unchanged
unabridged	unavailable	uncharitable
unacceptable	unavoidable	uncivilized
unaccom- panied	unaware	uncle

unclean		undaunted		understatement	
uncomfortable		undecided		understood	
uncommitted		undefended		understudy	
uncommon		undefined		undertake	
uncommuni-cative		undeniable		undertaken	
uncomplaining		under		undertone ·	
uncomplimen-tary		undercover		underwear	
uncompromis-ing		undercurrent		underwriter	
unconcern		undercut		undeserved	
unconcernedly		underestimate		undesirable	
unconditional		undergo		undeterred	
unconfirmed		undergraduate		undeveloped	
unconnected		underground		undid	
unconscious		undergrowth		undignified	
unconstitu-tional		underhand		undiluted	
uncontrollable		underline		undiminished	
unconventional		underlying		undischarged	
uncorrected		undermine		undisclosed	
uncouth		underneath		undiscovered	
uncover		underrate		undisguised	
uncultivated		undersigned		undismayed	
uncut		undersize		undisturbed	
undamaged		understand		undivided	
undated		understandably		undoubted	

199

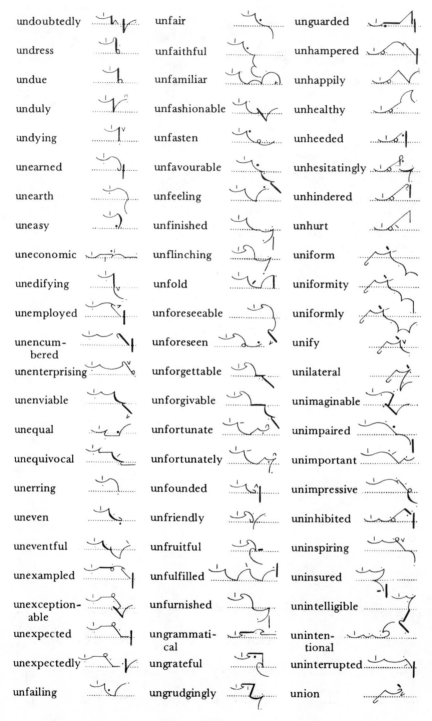

undoubtedly	unfair	unguarded
undress	unfaithful	unhampered
undue	unfamiliar	unhappily
unduly	unfashionable	unhealthy
undying	unfasten	unheeded
unearned	unfavourable	unhesitatingly
unearth	unfeeling	unhindered
uneasy	unfinished	unhurt
uneconomic	unflinching	uniform
unedifying	unfold	uniformity
unemployed	unforeseeable	uniformly
unencumbered	unforeseen	unify
unenterprising	unforgettable	unilateral
unenviable	unforgivable	unimaginable
unequal	unfortunate	unimpaired
unequivocal	unfortunately	unimportant
unerring	unfounded	unimpressive
uneven	unfriendly	uninhibited
uneventful	unfruitful	uninspiring
unexampled	unfulfilled	uninsured
unexceptionable	unfurnished	unintelligible
unexpected	ungrammatical	unintentional
unexpectedly	ungrateful	uninterrupted
unfailing	ungrudgingly	union

200

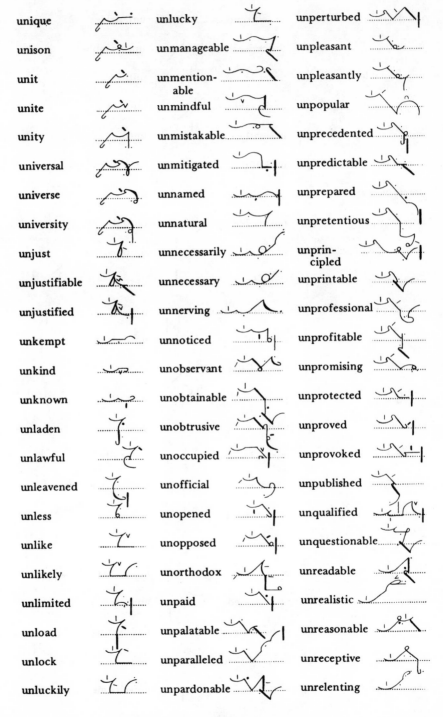

unique	unlucky	unperturbed
unison	unmanageable	unpleasant
unit	unmention-able	unpleasantly
unite	unmindful	unpopular
unity	unmistakable	unprecedented
universal	unmitigated	unpredictable
universe	unnamed	unprepared
university	unnatural	unpretentious
unjust	unnecessarily	unprin-cipled
unjustifiable	unnecessary	unprintable
unjustified	unnerving	unprofessional
unkempt	unnoticed	unprofitable
unkind	unobservant	unpromising
unknown	unobtainable	unprotected
unladen	unobtrusive	unproved
unlawful	unoccupied	unprovoked
unleavened	unofficial	unpublished
unless	unopened	unqualified
unlike	unopposed	unquestionable
unlikely	unorthodox	unreadable
unlimited	unpaid	unrealistic
unload	unpalatable	unreasonable
unlock	unparalleled	unreceptive
unluckily	unpardonable	unrelenting

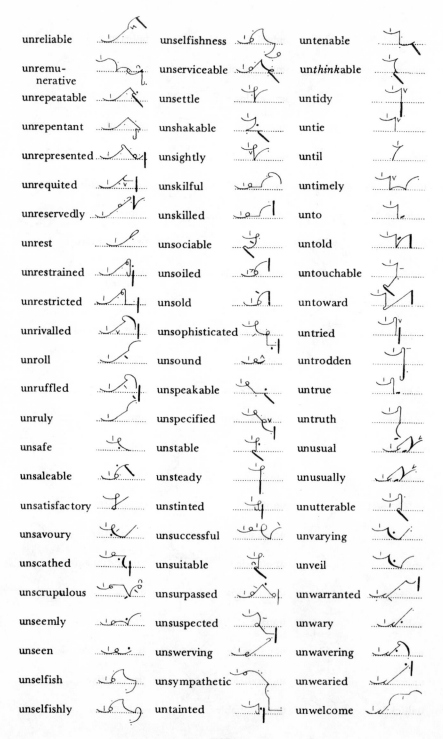

unreliable	unselfishness	untenable
unremu- nerative	unserviceable	un*think*able
unrepeatable	unsettle	untidy
unrepentant	unshakable	untie
unrepresented	unsightly	until
unrequited	unskilful	untimely
unreservedly	unskilled	unto
unrest	unsociable	untold
unrestrained	unsoiled	untouchable
unrestricted	unsold	untoward
unrivalled	unsophisticated	untried
unroll	unsound	untrodden
unruffled	unspeakable	untrue
unruly	unspecified	untruth
unsafe	unstable	unusual
unsaleable	unsteady	unusually
unsatisfactory	unstinted	unutterable
unsavoury	unsuccessful	unvarying
unscathed	unsuitable	unveil
unscrupulous	unsurpassed	unwarranted
unseemly	unsuspected	unwary
unseen	unswerving	unwavering
unselfish	unsympathetic	unwearied
unselfishly	untainted	unwelcome

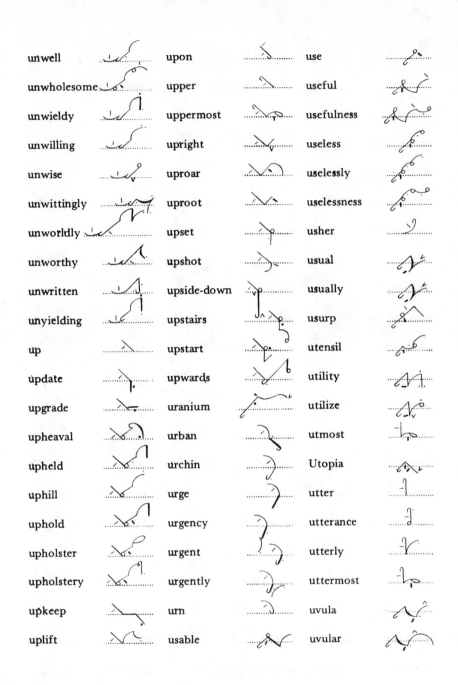

unwell	upon	use
unwholesome	upper	useful
unwieldy	uppermost	usefulness
unwilling	upright	useless
unwise	uproar	uselessly
unwittingly	uproot	uselessness
unworldly	upset	usher
unworthy	upshot	usual
unwritten	upside-down	usually
unyielding	upstairs	usurp
up	upstart	utensil
update	upwards	utility
upgrade	uranium	utilize
upheaval	urban	utmost
upheld	urchin	Utopia
uphill	urge	utter
uphold	urgency	utterance
upholster	urgent	utterly
upholstery	urgently	uttermost
upkeep	urn	uvula
uplift	usable	uvular

V

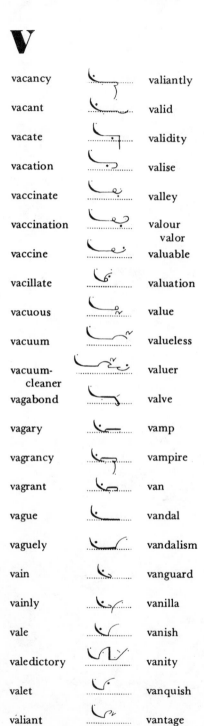
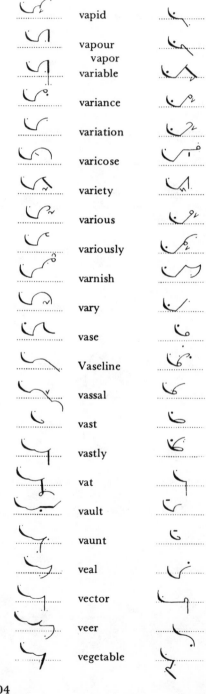

vacancy	valiantly	vapid	
vacant	valid	vapour vapor	
vacate	validity	variable	
vacation	valise	variance	
vaccinate	valley	variation	
vaccination	valour valor	varicose	
vaccine	valuable	variety	
vacillate	valuation	various	
vacuous	value	variously	
vacuum	valueless	varnish	
vacuum-cleaner	valuer	vary	
vagabond	valve	vase	
vagary	vamp	Vaseline	
vagrancy	vampire	vassal	
vagrant	van	vast	
vague	vandal	vastly	
vaguely	vandalism	vat	
vain	vanguard	vault	
vainly	vanilla	vaunt	
vale	vanish	veal	
valedictory	vanity	vector	
valet	vanquish	veer	
valiant	vantage	vegetable	

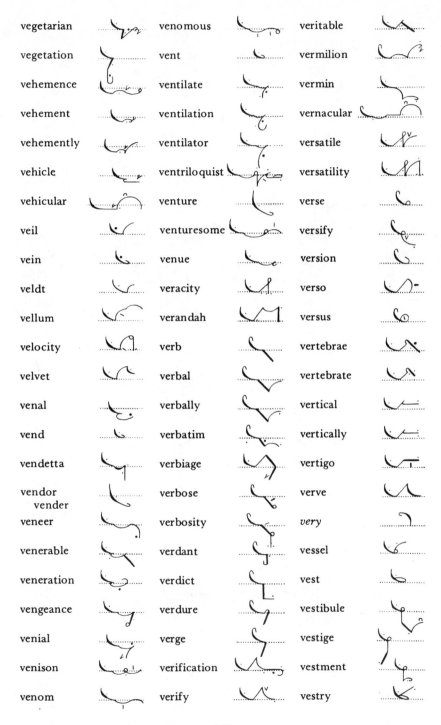

vegetarian	venomous	veritable
vegetation	vent	vermilion
vehemence	ventilate	vermin
vehement	ventilation	vernacular
vehemently	ventilator	versatile
vehicle	ventriloquist	versatility
vehicular	venture	verse
veil	venturesome	versify
vein	venue	version
veldt	veracity	verso
vellum	verandah	versus
velocity	verb	vertebrae
velvet	verbal	vertebrate
venal	verbally	vertical
vend	verbatim	vertically
vendetta	verbiage	vertigo
vendor vender	verbose	verve
veneer	verbosity	very
venerable	verdant	vessel
veneration	verdict	vest
vengeance	verdure	vestibule
venial	verge	vestige
venison	verification	vestment
venom	verify	vestry

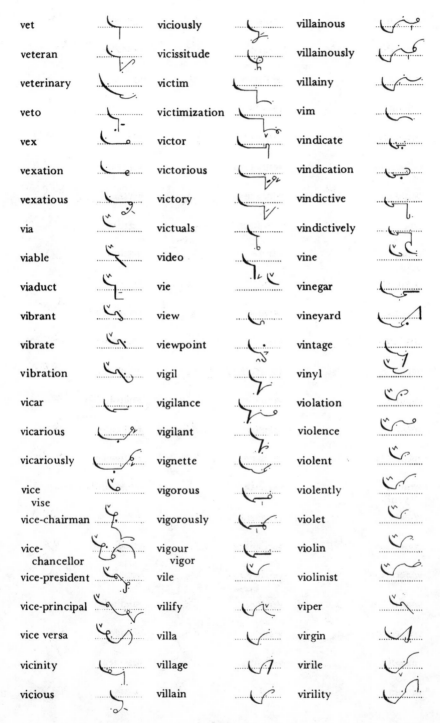

vet	viciously	villainous
veteran	vicissitude	villainously
veterinary	victim	villainy
veto	victimization	vim
vex	victor	vindicate
vexation	victorious	vindication
vexatious	victory	vindictive
via	victuals	vindictively
viable	video	vine
viaduct	vie	vinegar
vibrant	view	vineyard
vibrate	viewpoint	vintage
vibration	vigil	vinyl
vicar	vigilance	violation
vicarious	vigilant	violence
vicariously	vignette	violent
vice vise	vigorous	violently
vice-chairman	vigorously	violet
vice-chancellor	vigour vigor	violin
vice-president	vile	violinist
vice-principal	vilify	viper
vice versa	villa	virgin
vicinity	village	virile
vicious	villain	virility

206

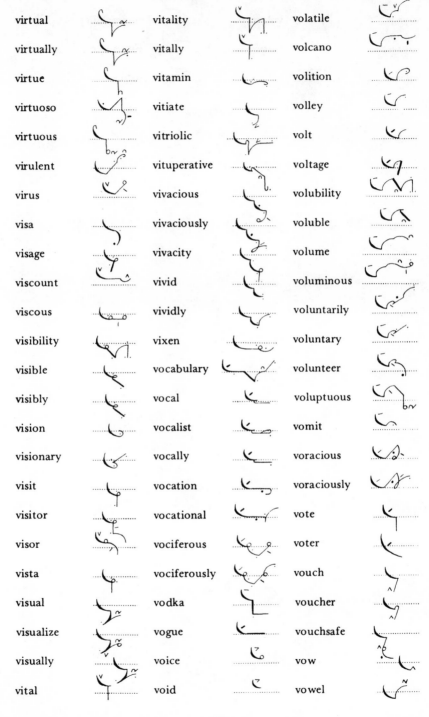

virtual	vitality	volatile
virtually	vitally	volcano
virtue	vitamin	volition
virtuoso	vitiate	volley
virtuous	vitriolic	volt
virulent	vituperative	voltage
virus	vivacious	volubility
visa	vivaciously	voluble
visage	vivacity	volume
viscount	vivid	voluminous
viscous	vividly	voluntarily
visibility	vixen	voluntary
visible	vocabulary	volunteer
visibly	vocal	voluptuous
vision	vocalist	vomit
visionary	vocally	voracious
visit	vocation	voraciously
visitor	vocational	vote
visor	vociferous	voter
vista	vociferously	vouch
visual	vodka	voucher
visualize	vogue	vouchsafe
visually	voice	vow
vital	void	vowel

voyage	![shorthand]	vulgar	![shorthand]	vulnerability	![shorthand]
voyager	![shorthand]	vulgarity	![shorthand]	vulnerable	![shorthand]
vulcanize	![shorthand]	vulgarly	![shorthand]	vulture	![shorthand]

wad	wallet	warfare
wade	wallop	warily
wafer	wallow	warlike
waffle	wallpaper	warm
waft	walnut	warmer
wag	walrus	warmest
wage	waltz	warm-hearted
wager	wan	warmly
wagon waggon	wand	warmth
waif	wander	warn
wail	wane	warp
waist	wangle	warrant
waistline	want	warranty
wait	wanton	warren
waiter	wantonly	warrior
waitress	war	warship
waive	warble	wart
waiver	ward	wary
wake	warden	was
waken	warder	wash
walk	wardrobe	washer
walker	warehouse	washing-up
wall	wares	wasp

wastage		waxen		wearily		
waste		way		wearisome		
wasteful		waybill		weary		
wastefully		wayfarer		weather		
wastrel		waylay		weave		
watch		wayside		weaver		
watcher		wayward		web		
watchful		we		wed		
watchman		weak		wedding		
water		weaken		wedge		
waterfall		weaker		Wednesday		
waterlogged		weakest		weed		
watermark		weakly		week		
watermelon		weakness		weekday		
waterproof		weal		weekend		
watershed		wealth		weekly		
watertight		wealthier		weep		
waterway		wealthiest		weigh		
waterworks		wealthy		weight		
watery		wean		weightily		
watt		weapon		weighty		
wave		wear		weird		
wavy		wearable		welcome		
wax		wearer		weld		

210

welfare	welfare	westward	westward	whereon	whereon
well		wet		wheresoever	
well-balanced		whack		whereto	
well-*be*ing		whale		whereupon	
well-bred		wharf		wherever	
well-disposed		wharfinger		wherewithal	
well-informed		what		whether	
well-known		whatever		*which*	
well-meaning		whatsoever		*which*ever	
well-meant		wheat		whiff	
well-off		wheatsheaf		while	
well-read		wheel		whilst	
well-spoken		wheelbarrow		whim	
well-timed		wheelchair		whimper	
well-wisher		when		whimsical	
welt		whence		whimsically	
wench		whenever		whine	
wend		where		whip	
went		whereabouts		whirl	
wept		whereas		whirlpool	
were		whereby		whirlwind	
west		wherefore		whisk	
westerly		where*in*		whisky whiskey	
western		where*of*		whisper	

211

whist	wide	wilt
whistle	widely	wily
white	widen	win
whitewash	wider	wince
whither	widespread	winch
whittle	widest	wind, *n*
whiz	widow	wind, *v*
who	widower	windmill
*who*ever	width	window
whole	wield	windscreen
wholehearted	wife	windward
whole-heartedly	wig	windy
wholesale	wild	wine
wholesome	wilder	wineglass
wholly	wilderness	wing
whom	wildest	wink
whoop	wildly	winner
whose	wilful	winsome
whosoever	wilfully	winsomely
why	wilfulness	winter
wick	*will*	wintry
wicked	willingly *or*	wipe
wickerwork	willingness *or*	wiper
wicket	willow	wire

wiry		withstood		woo
wisdom		witless		wood
wise		witness		wooden
wisely		witticism		woodland
wiser		wittily		woodwork
wisest		wittingly		wool
wish		witty		woollen woolen
wishful		wives		woolly
wistful		wizard		word
wistfully		wizened		wore
wit		wobble		work
witch		woke		worker
with		wolf		workman
withal		woman		workmanship
withdraw		womanhood		workshop
withdrawal		womanly		world
withdrawn		women		worldly
withdrew		won		worldwide
wither		wonder		worm
withheld		*wonderful*		worn
withhold		*wonderfully*		worry
within		wonderingly		worse
without		wondrous		worship
withstand		won't		worst

213

worsted	wreak	writ	
worth	wreath	write	
worthier	wreathe	write-off	
worthiest	wreck	writer	
worthily	wreckage	write-up	
worthless	wrench	writhe	
worthwhile	wrestle	written	
worthy	wretch	wrong	
would	wretched	wrongdoer	
wound, *n*	wretchedness	wrong*doing*	
wound, *v*	wriggle	wrongful	
wove	wrily	wrongfully	
woven	wring	wrongly	
wrangle	wringer	wrote	
wrap	wrinkle	wrought	
wrapper	wrist	wrung	
wrath	wristlet	wry	
wrathful	wristwatch	wyvern	

X

xenophobia   X-ray   xylophone

xerox xylonite xylophonist

Y

yacht		yes		young	
yank		yesman		younger	
yap		yesterday		youngest	
yard		yet		youngster	
yarn		yew		*your*	
year		yield		*yours*	
*year*book		yodel		*yourself*	
yearly		yoga		*yourselves*	
yearn		yoke		youth	
yeast		yokel		youthful	
yell		yolk		youthfulness	
yellow		yonder		yuletide	
yelp		*you*		yo-yo	

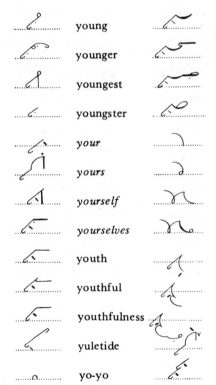

Z

zeal		zero		zodiac	
zealot		zest		zone	
zealous		zigzag		zoological	
zealously		zinc		zoologist	
zebra		zipper		zoology	
zenith		zircon		zoom	
zephyr		zither		zoonomy	

List of Proper Names

Abraham		Bertha		Daniel			
Adams		Betty		David			
Agnes		Brenda		Davis			
Aileen		Brian		Den(n)is			
Albert		Bruce		Derek			
Al(l)an		Bryant		Diana			
Alexander		Buchanan		Donald			
Andrew		Campbell		Dorothy			
Angela		Carol		Edward			
Ann(e)		Caroline		Edwin			
Ant(h)ony		Catherine		Eileen			
Armstrong		Charles		Eleanor			
Arnold		Christopher		Elizabeth			
Arthur		Clara		Emerson			
Barbara		Clarence		Eric			
Beatrice		Clark		Ernest			
Benjamin		Cynthia		Ethel			

217

Fillmore		Jacqueline		Louis	
Frances		James		Louise	
Francis		Jane		Luther	
Frank		Janet		Lynne	
Fraser		Jean		Mackenzie	
Frederick		Jennifer		Malcolm	
Geoffrey		Jeremy		Margaret	
George		Jessie (Jesse)		Margery	
Gerald		Jill		Marilyn	
Gertrude		John		Marion	
Gillian		Johnson		Marjorie	
Gordon		Jonathan		Marshall	
Harold		Joseph		Martin	
Harriet		Julia		Maureen	
Hazel		Katherine		Maurice	
Helen		Kathleen		Michael	
Henry		Kenneth		Moira	
Herbert		Lawrence		Moore	
Howard		Leonard		Morris	
Hugh		Lesley		Nancy	
Ia(i)n		Leslie		Napolean	
Irving		Lewis		Neil	
Isaac		Lillian		Nelson	
Isabel		Linda		Nic(h)olas	

218

Nigel		Raymond		Shakespeare	
Norman		Richard		Sharon	
Oliver		Richardson		Sheila	
Olivia		Robert		Sidney	
Owen		Roger		Simon	
Patricia		Ro(w)land		Smith	
Patrick		Rosamund		Stephanie	
Paul		Roy		Stephen (Steven)	
Pauline		Rupert		Stewart (Stuart)	
Peggy		Russell		Susan	
Peter		Ruth		T(h)eresa	
Philip		Samuel		Thomas	
Phyllis		Sarah		Tracey	
Rachel		Seamus		William	
Ralph		Sean		Wilson	

List of World Place Names

Abyssinia		Algonquin		Asia	
Adelaide		Allegheny		Athabasca	
Aden		Allentown		Athens	
Afghanistan		Altoona		Atlanta	
Africa		America		Atlantic	
Ajax		Amherst		Atlantic City	
Akron		Amman		Augusta	
Alabama		Amsterdam		Aurora	
Alaska		Angola		Austin	
Albania		Annapolis		Australia	
Albany		Antigua		Austria	
Alberta		Arabia			
Albuquerque		Arctic		**Bahamas**	
Alexander		Argentina		Baghdad	
Alexandria		Arizona		Baltic	
Alfred		Arkansas		Baltimore	
Algeria		Armenia		Banff	

220

Bangkok	Bolivia	Brussels	
Bangladesh	Bombay	Bryant	
Barbados	Bonn	Bucharest	
Barcelona	Borneo	Budapest	
Barrie	Boston	Buffalo	
Bathurst	Boulder	Buenos Aires	
Baton Rouge	Brampton	Bulgaria	
Bavaria	Brandon	Bunker Hill	
Bayonne	Brantford	Burgundy	
Bedford	Brasilia	Burlington	
Beirut	Brazil	Burma	
Belfast	Brazilian	Butte	
Belgium	Bremen		
Belgrade	Bridgeport	Cairo	
Belleville	Brisbane	Calcutta	
Berkeley	Britain	Calgary	
Berlin	British Columbia	California	
Bermuda	Briton	Cambodia	
Berne	Brittany	Cambridge	
Bethlehem	Broadway	Camden	
Binghamton	Brockville	Campbellton	
Birmingham	Bronx	Canberra	
Bismarck	Brooklyn	Canada	
Boise	Brunei	Canadian	

Canton	Cologne	Danzig
Capetown	Colombia	Dar es Salaam
Capitol	Colombian	Dartmouth
Caracas	Colorado	Davenport
Caribbean	Columbus	Darwin
Carolina	Concord	Dayton
Carson City	Connecticut	Dawson Creek
Casablanca	Coolidge	Delaware
Catskill	Cornell	Delhi (India)
Cedar Rapids	Corner Brook	Delhi (N.A.)
Charlotte	Cornwall	Denmark
Charlottetown	Corsica	Denver
Chatam	Costa Rica	Des Moines
Chattanooga	Covington	Detroit
Chautauqua	Cranbrook	Dominica
Cheyenne	Cuba	Dorchester
Chicago	Crete	Dover
Chile	Cypriot	Dresden
Chilean	Cyprus	Dublin
China	Czecho-slovakia	Duluth
Chinese		Dundas
Cincinnati	Dallas	Durban
Cleveland	Damascus	Durham
Cobourg	Danish	Dutch

222

East Indies		Finland		Georgia	
East Kildonan		Flin Flon		Geraldton	
Ecuador		Flint		German	
Edgar		Florence		Germany	
Edinburgh		Florida		Glace Bay	
Edmonton		Formosa		Glasgow	
Edmundston		Fort Erie		Grande Prairie	
Egypt		Fort Wayne		Grand Rapids	
Egyptian		Fort Worth		Great Britain	
El Paso		France		Great Falls	
England		Frankfort		Greece	
English		Fredericton		Greek	
Erie		French		Greenland	
Ethiopia		Fresno		Greenwich	
Euphrates		Fulton		Grimsby	
Europe				Guatemala	
European		Galt		Guam	
Evanston		Galveston		Guelph	
Evansville		Garfield			
Everest		Gary		Hague	
		Gaspe		Haiti	
Fall River		Geneva		Halifax	
Fargo		Genoa		Hanoi	
Fiji		Georgetown		Hamburg	

Hamilton

Harding

Harlem

Harrisburg

Harrison

Hartford

Harvard

Havana

Hawaii

Hayes

Helena

Helsinki

Holland

Hollywood

Honduras

Hong Kong

Honolulu

Hoover

Houston

Hudson

Hugh

Hull

Hungary

Huntington

Huronia

Iceland

Idaho

Illinois

India

Indiana

Indianapolis

Indonesia

Iowa

Iran

Ireland

Irish

Islington

Israel

Istanbul

Italian

Italy

Iraq

Jackson

Jacksonville

Jamaica

Japan

Japanese

Jeferson City

Jersey City

Johannes-
burg

Jerusalem

Johnstown

Jordan

Juneau

Kamloops

Kansas

Kansas City

Kapuskasing

Kashmir

Kelowna

Kenora

Kentucky

Kenya

Kiev

Kingston

Kitchener

Knoxville

Kobe

Korea

224

Kuwait		Liverpool		Manila	
		London		Manitoba	
Labrador		Long Beach		Markham	
Lafayette		Long Island		Marseilles	
Lagos		Longueuil		Maryland	
Lake Superior		Los Angeles		Massachusetts	
Lansing		Louisiana		McKeesport	
Laos		Louisville		McKinley	
La Salle		Lowell		Medicine Hat	
Laval		Lusaka		Mediterranean	
Leamington		Luxembourg		Melbourne	
Lebanon				Memphis	
Leeds		Macon		Mexico	
Leipzig		Madagascar		Mexico City	
Leningrad		Madeira		Miami	
Lethbridge		Madison		Michigan	
Lexington		Madras		Midland	
Liberia		Madrid		Milan	
Libya		Maine		Milwaukee	
Lima		Malaya		Minneapolis	
Lincoln		Malta		Minnesota	
Lindsay		Manchester		Miquelon	
Lisbon		Manchuria		Mississauga	
Little Rock		Manhattan		Mississippi	

225

Missouri	Naples	New Zealand
Mobile	Nashville	Newmarket
Mohawk	Nassau	Newark
Monaco	Natal	Newfoundland
Moncton	Nebraska	Newport
Mongolia	Nelson	Niagara
Monroe	Nepal	Niagara Falls
Monrovia	Netherlands	Niagara-on-the-Lake
Montana	Nevada	Nicaragua
Montevideo	New Bedford	Niger
Montgomery	New Brunswick	Nigeria
Montpelier	New Delhi	Nile
Montserrat _or_	New Glasgow	Norfolk
Montreal	New Guinea	Normandy
Moore	New Hampshire	North America
Moose Jaw	New Haven	North Battleford
Morocco	New Jersey	North Bay
Moscow	New Mexico	North Carolina
Mount Vernon	New Orleans	North Dakota
Munich	New Rochelle	North Vancouver
	New Westminister	Northern Ireland
Nairobi	New York	Northwest Territories
Nanaimo	New York City	Norway
Nanking	New York State	Norwegian

226

Nova Scotia		Pakistan		Poland	
		Palermo		Polish	
Oakland		Palestine		Polk	
Oakville		Panama		Pontiac	
Ohio		Paraguay		Portage la Prairie	
Oklahoma		Paris		Port Alberni	
Olympic		Pasadena		Port Colborne	
Olympia		Passaic		Port Coquitlam	
Omaha		Paterson		Port Moody	
Oman		Peace River		Portland	
Ontario		Peking		Portsmouth	
Oregon		Pembroke		Portugal	
Orient		Pennsyl- vania		Potomac	
Orillia		Penticton		Prague	
Orlando		Peoria		Preston	
Oromocto		Perth		Prince Albert	
Osaka		Peru		Prince Edward Island	
Oslo		Peterborough		Prince George	
Oshawa		Philadelphia		Prince Rupert	
Ottawa		Phillippines		Providence	
Owen Sound		Phoenix		Puerto Rico	
Oxford		Pierre			
		Pittsburg			
Pacific		Plymouth		Quebec	

227

Queensland	Sacramento	San Francisco
Queenstown	Saigon	San Jose
	Saint John	San Juan
Rabat	St. Albert	Santa Fe
Racine	St. Boniface	Santiago
Raleigh	St. Catherines	Sardinia
Reading	St. James Assiniboia	Sarnia
Red Deer	St. John's	Saskatchewan
Red River	St. Lawrence	Saskatoon
Regina	St. Louis	Saudi Arabia
Reno	St. Lucia	Sault Ste. Marie
Rhine	St. Paul	Savannah
Rhode Island	St. Petersburg	Schenectady
Rhodesia	St. Pierre	Scotch
Richmond	St. Thomas	Scotland
Richmond Hill	St. Vincent	Scottish
Rio de Janeiro	St. Vital	Scranton
Rochester	Salem	Seattle
Rocky Mountains	Salisbury	Selkirk
Rome	Salt Lake City	Senegal
Roosevelt	Salvador	Seoul
Rotterdam	Samoa	Shanghai
Romania	San Antonio	Sheffield
Russia	San Diego	Sherbrooke

Shreveport	Stratford	Tel-Aviv
Siam	Sudan	Tennessee
Siberia	Sudbury	Terre Haute
Sicily	Suez	Texas
Simcoe	Suffolk	Thailand
Singapore	Sumatra	Thompson
Sioux City	Summerside	Thorold
Somalia	Swede	Thunder Bay
Somerville	Sweden	Tibet
South Africa	Swift Current	Timmins
South America	Swiss	Tokyo
South Bend	Switzerland	Toledo
South Carolina	Sydney	Topeka
South Dakota	Syracuse	Toronto
Southampton	Syria	Transcona
Soviet Russia		Transvaal
Spain	Tacoma	Trenton
Spaniard	Taft	Trinidad
Spanish	Taiwan	Tripoli
Spokane	Tallahassie	Trois Rivieres
Springfield	Tampa	Troy
Stalingrad	Tanzania	Tucson
Stamford	Tasmania	Tulsa
Stockholm	Teheran	Tunisia

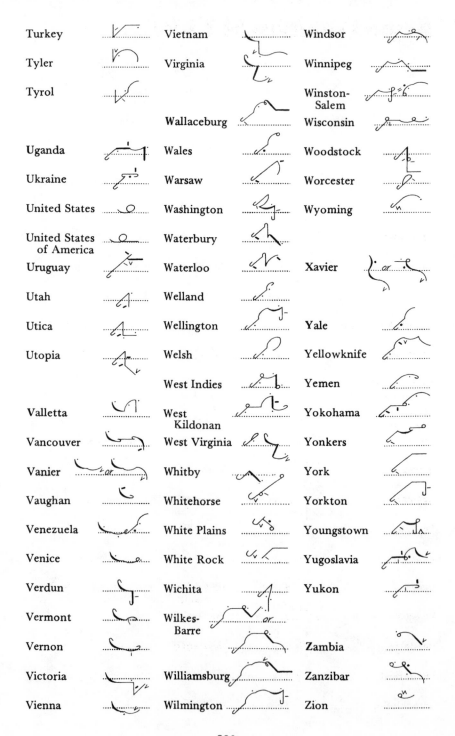

Turkey	Vietnam	Windsor
Tyler	Virginia	Winnipeg
Tyrol		Winston-Salem
	Wallaceburg	Wisconsin
Uganda	Wales	Woodstock
Ukraine	Warsaw	Worcester
United States	Washington	Wyoming
United States of America	Waterbury	
Uruguay	Waterloo	Xavier
Utah	Welland	
Utica	Wellington	Yale
Utopia	Welsh	Yellowknife
	West Indies	Yemen
Valletta	West Kildonan	Yokohama
Vancouver	West Virginia	Yonkers
Vanier	Whitby	York
Vaughan	Whitehorse	Yorkton
Venezuela	White Plains	Youngstown
Venice	White Rock	Yugoslavia
Verdun	Wichita	Yukon
Vermont	Wilkes-Barre	
Vernon		Zambia
Victoria	Williamsburg	Zanzibar
Vienna	Wilmington	Zion

230

Some Common SI Units

Angstrom

ampere

candela

centimetre

coulomb

cubic metre

degree
  Celcius

farad

gram

hectare

henry

joule

kelvin

kilogram

kilohertz

kilojoule

kilometre

kiloohm

kilopascal

kilosecond

kilovolt

kilowatt

kilowatt
  hour

litre

megahertz

megajoule

megaohm

megavolt

metre

metre per
  second

microampere

micrometre

microsecond

milliampere

milligram		ohm	
millimetre		pascal	
milliohm		picometre	
millisecond		square metre	
millivolt		tesla	
mole		volt	
nanometre		watt	
newton		weber	

List of Pitman Pacers

a/an		dear		how	
able to		do		I/eye	
accord/according/ according to		dollar/had		immediate	
all		enlarge		immediately	
almost		enlarged		in/any	
also		enlargement		influence	
altogether		eye/I		influenced	
always		for		influential	
and		gentleman		information	
any/in		gentlemen		is/his	
anything		had/dollar		it	
are		has/as		January	
as/has		have		large	
be		he		largely	
before		his/is		larger	
but		hour/our		largest	
cannot		hours		manufacture	

manufactured	satisfactory	too
manufacturing	several	two
manufacturer	shall	United States
manufactures	should	United States of America
more	something	very
nevertheless	thank	we
New York	that	which
nothing	the	who
notwithstanding	their	will
of	there	without
oh/owe	therefore	wonderful/ly
on	thing	would
our/hour	think	year
ours	this	yesterday
owe/oh	this is	you
owing	to/too/two	your
put	today	yours
responsible	to be	yourself
responsibility	together	yours sincerely

6 7 8 000315 82 81 80